Key Stage 3

Modern Britain

1760–1900

Robert Peal

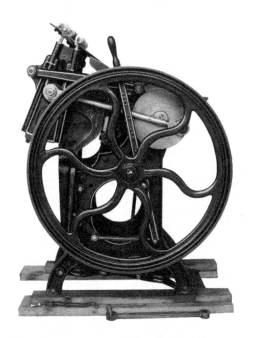

William Collins' dream of knowledge for all began with the publication of his first book in 1819. A self-educated mill worker, he not only enriched millions of lives, but also founded a flourishing publishing house. Today, staying true to this spirit, Collins books are packed with inspiration, innovation and practical expertise. They place you at the centre of a world of possibility and give you exactly what you need to explore it.

Collins. Freedom to teach

Published by Collins
An imprint of HarperCollins*Publishers*
The News Building
1 London Bridge Street
London SE1 9GF

HarperCollins*Publishers*
1st Floor, Watermarque Building, Ringsend Road
Dublin 4, Ireland

10 9

ISBN 978-0-00-819525-0

A catalogue record for this book is available from the British Library

Publisher: Katie Sergeant
Editor: Hannah Dove
Author: Robert Peal
Fact-checker: Barbara Hibbert
Copy-editor: Sally Clifford
Image researcher: Alison Prior
Proof-reader: Ros and Chris Davies
Cover designer: Angela English
Cover image: typografie/Alamy
Production controller: Rachel Weaver
Typesetter: QBS
Printed and Bound in the UK using 100% Renewable Electricity at CPI Group (UK) Ltd

MIX
Paper from
responsible sources
FSC™ C007454

FSC™ is a non-profit international organisation established to promote the responsible management of the world's forests. Products carrying the FSC label are independently certified to assure consumers that they come from forests that are managed to meet the social, economic and ecological needs of present and future generations, and other controlled sources.

Find out more about HarperCollins and the environment at
www.harpercollins.co.uk/green

Contents

Introduction

'We who have lived before railways were made, belong to another world…It was only yesterday; but what a gulf between now and then! Then was the old world. Stage-coaches, more or less swift, riding-horses, pack-horses, highwaymen, knights in armour, Norman invaders, Roman legions, Druids, Ancient Britons painted blue, and so forth…But your railroad starts the new era.'

William Makepeace Thackeray, *Cornhill Magazine*, 1860

It is difficult to think of a more transformative period of British history than the seventy years from 1760 to 1830. This period saw Britain gain a global empire following the Seven Years War, colonise India, settle Australia, lose the American War of Independence, abolish the slave trade, and fight in the campaign to defeat the French Emperor Napoleon Bonaparte.

This period also saw the birth of the steam engine and the Industrial Revolution, causing the rapid growth of industrial cities such as Manchester, Birmingham and Leeds. Britain transformed from a rural to an urban nation, and its economy grew at a speed unimaginable to previous generations.

By the early 19th century, a combination of industry and empire had made Britain the most powerful nation in the world. From 1837 to 1901, a woman whose name became synonymous with an entire era ruled Britain: Queen Victoria.

Victorian Britain was a place of self-assurance, with a deep faith in economic growth, social reform and Imperial rule. By 1901, this confidence was beginning to unravel. Queen Victoria had died, Britain's industrial leadership had been challenged, and the Boer War was tarnishing the moral standing of the British Empire.

The world today is as it is because of what has happened in the past. In studying history you may even start to see events in the present mirroring events in the past. As it is often said, history does not repeat itself, but it does sometimes rhyme.

Robert Peal, author of *Knowing History*

Concise chapter introductions set the scene and focus your learning.

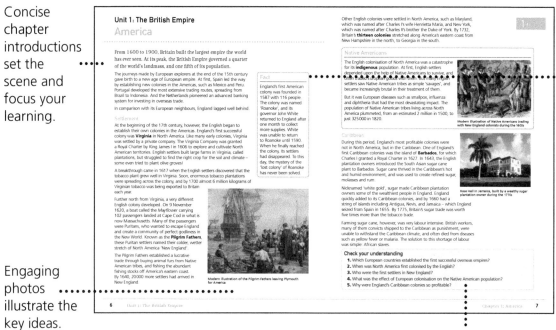

Fact boxes provide bite-sized details.

Engaging photos illustrate the key ideas.

End-of-chapter questions are designed to check and consolidate your understanding.

Timelines map out the key dates from the unit, and help you understand the course of events.

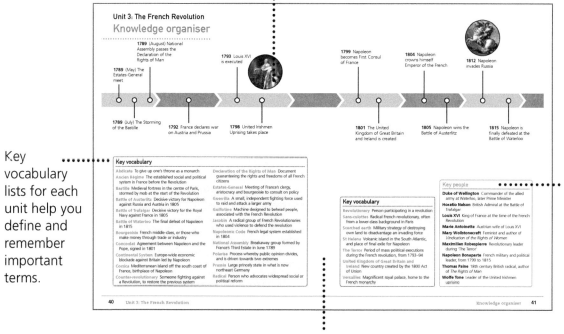

Key vocabulary lists for each unit help you define and remember important terms.

Key people boxes summarise the key figures of the time.

Knowledge organisers can be used to revise and quiz yourself on key dates, definitions and descriptions.

America

From 1600 to 1900, Britain built the largest empire the world has ever seen. At its peak, the British Empire governed a quarter of the world's landmass, and one fifth of its population.

The journeys made by European explorers at the end of the 15th century gave birth to a new age of European empire. At first, Spain led the way by establishing new colonies in the Americas, such as Mexico and Peru. Portugal developed the most extensive trading routes, spreading from Brazil to Indonesia. And the Netherlands pioneered an advanced banking system for investing in overseas trade.

In comparison with its European neighbours, England lagged well behind.

Settlement

At the beginning of the 17th century, however, the English began to establish their own colonies in the Americas. England's first successful colony was **Virginia** in North America. Like many early colonies, Virginia was settled by a private company. The Virginia Company was granted a Royal Charter by King James I in 1606 to explore and cultivate North American territories. English settlers built large farms in Virginia, called plantations, but struggled to find the right crop for the soil and climate – some even tried to plant olive groves!

A breakthrough came in 1617 when the English settlers discovered that the tobacco plant grew well in Virginia. Soon, enormous tobacco plantations were spreading across the colony, and by 1700 almost 6 million kilograms of Virginian tobacco was being exported to Britain each year.

Further north from Virginia, a very different English colony developed. On 9 November 1620, a boat called the *Mayflower* carrying 102 passengers landed at Cape Cod in what is now Massachusetts. Many of the passengers were Puritans, who wanted to escape England and create a community of perfect godliness in the New World. Known as the **Pilgrim Fathers**, these Puritan settlers named their colder, wetter stretch of North America 'New England'.

The Pilgrim Fathers established a lucrative trade through buying animal furs from Native American tribes, and fishing the abundant fishing stocks off America's eastern coast. By 1640, 20000 more settlers had arrived in New England.

> **Fact**
>
> England's first American colony was founded in 1587 with 116 people. The colony was named 'Roanoke', and its governor John White returned to England after one month to collect more supplies. White was unable to return to Roanoke until 1590. When he finally reached the colony, its settlers had disappeared. To this day, the mystery of the 'lost colony' of Roanoke has never been solved.

Modern illustration of the Pilgrim Fathers leaving Plymouth for America

Other English colonies were settled in North America, such as Maryland, which was named after Charles I's wife Henrietta Maria, and New York, which was named after Charles II's brother the Duke of York. By 1732, Britain's **thirteen colonies** stretched along America's eastern coast from New Hampshire in the north, to Georgia in the south.

Native Americans

The English colonisation of North America was a catastrophe for its **indigenous** population. At first, English settlers depended upon the help of Native Americans to survive, and often traded European goods with them. But many English settlers saw Native American tribes as simple 'savages', and became increasingly brutal in their treatment of them.

But it was European diseases such as smallpox, influenza and diphtheria that had the most devastating impact. The population of Native American tribes living across North America plummeted, from an estimated 2 million in 1500, to just 325 000 in 1820.

Modern illustration of Native Americans trading with New England colonists during the 1600s

Caribbean

During this period, England's most profitable colonies were not in North America, but in the Caribbean. One of England's first Caribbean colonies was the island of **Barbados**, for which Charles I granted a Royal Charter in 1627. In 1643, the English plantation owners introduced the South Asian sugar cane plant to Barbados. Sugar cane thrived in the Caribbean's hot and humid environment, and was used to create refined sugar, molasses and rum.

Rose Hall in Jamaica, built by a wealthy sugar plantation owner during the 1770s

Nicknamed 'white gold', sugar made Caribbean plantation owners some of the wealthiest people in England. England quickly added to its Caribbean colonies, and by 1660 had a string of islands including Antigua, Nevis, and Jamaica – which England seized from Spain in 1655. By 1775, Britain's sugar trade was worth five times more than the tobacco trade.

Farming sugar cane, however, was very labour intensive. British workers, many of them convicts shipped to the Caribbean as punishment, were unable to withstand the Caribbean climate, and often died from diseases such as yellow fever or malaria. The solution to this shortage of labour was simple: African slaves.

Check your understanding

1. Which European countries established the first successful overseas empires?
2. When was North America first colonised by the English?
3. Who were the first settlers in New England?
4. What was the effect of European colonisation on the Native American population?
5. Why were England's Caribbean colonies so profitable?

India

During the 16th century, European merchants began trading directly with what was perhaps the world's wealthiest region: India.

The Red Fort, centre of Mughal rule in India

At this time, most of the Indian subcontinent was ruled by the Mughal Emperor. The **Mughals** were originally Muslim warlords from Central Asia, who conquered India during the 1550s. The Mughal Emperor granted each province of India to a prince, known as a *nawab*, to rule on his behalf.

European merchants competed for their share of the valuable trade in Indian sugar, saltpetre, indigo dye, and – most importantly – high-quality cotton and silk. However, European merchants first had to gain permission from the Mughal Emperor and his local *nawab*. First the Portuguese, then the Dutch, and finally the English and French were all given permission to trade, and built fortified trading posts known as **factories** along India's coastline.

In 1600, Queen Elizabeth gave a royal charter to the **East India Company**. Over the course of the 17th century, the East India Company was given permission to trade in India at three major factories: Bombay (Mumbai) in India's northwest, Madras (Chennai) in the southeast, and Calcutta (Kolkata) in the northeastern province of **Bengal**. Unlike the settler colonies of the Americas, the East India Company's factories were built solely for trade. British merchants paid little attention to the interior of the vast country that lay beyond their coastal fortresses.

Diamond Pitt

Thomas Pitt travelled to India in 1674 to make his fortune. Despite working for the East India Company, he conducted his own private trade outside company business. In 1701, Pitt acquired a 410-carat diamond, then the largest in the world, and sold it in 1717 to the French royal family for five times its original price. Merchants who made their fortune in India were nicknamed 'nabobs', and this deal made 'Diamond Pitt' one of the richest nabobs in England.

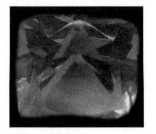

Fact

The Mughal Emperor governed India from the Red Fort in Delhi, where he sat on a magnificent golden throne. The back of the throne represented an unfolding peacock tail, encrusted with rubies, diamonds and other precious stones.

British expansion

By the 1740s, the central power of the Mughal Emperor in India was breaking down. Afghan armies were invading India from the North, and across India, *nawabs* were breaking from Mughal authority and establishing their own independent kingdoms.

In response to this confusion, the East India Company began to fortify its coastal factories. The Company built its own army, recruiting troops from India's warrior castes and British officers to lead them. During the 1750s, the Company became involved in the power struggles of competing Indian nawabs, often fighting battles against rival *nawabs* backed by the French East India Company.

In 1756, Bengal gained a new *nawab*, Siraj ud-Daulah, who resented the growing size of Calcutta, Britain's trading port in Bengal. In June 1756, Siraj seized Calcutta from the British. News of the loss of Calcutta spread south to Madras, where an ambitious young army officer in the East India Company Army named Robert Clive decided to take action.

Clive marched his army 1000 miles north from Madras to relieve Calcutta. A canny politician as well as a talented soldier, Clive persuaded Siraj's commander, Mir Jafar, to betray his own *nawab*. At the **Battle of Plassey** on 23 June, 1757, Clive's combination of Indian soldiers and European weapons proved brutally effective. With just 3000 troops, he defeated Siraj's army of 50 000 men. Clive then installed Mir Jafar as a 'puppet' *nawab* of Bengal.

Contemporary painting of Robert Clive meeting with Mir Jafar after the Battle of Plassey

At the **Treaty of Allahabad** in 1765, the Mughal Emperor placed the province of Bengal under the direct rule of the East India Company, with Robert Clive as Governor. This turning point marks the beginning of the British Empire in India. It gave the East India Company the right to tax 20 million people, making around £3 million a year. For the Company, territory and taxation would prove to be even more profitable than trade.

Following the Treaty of Allahabad, the East India Company Army grew to over 100 000 men, and continued to expand the boundaries of its power across India. This process was driven by opportunistic army officers, such as Clive, who acted with a great deal of independence from the British government and company directors back in London – many of whom were opposed to the growing political power of the East India Company.

By 1815, the East India Company ruled much of northeast India, spreading from Bengal towards Delhi; the entire eastern coast from Calcutta in the north to the Carnatic in the south; and a growing portion of southwest India. Around 40 million Indians were living directly under British rule, including – from 1803 onwards – the Mughal Emperor himself. In the place of the crumbling Mughal Empire, the Governor General of the East India Company was now the *de facto* ruler of much of India.

Statue of Robert Clive in Whitehall, London

Check your understanding

1. Who ruled India during the 16th and 17th centuries?
2. Where did the East India Company conduct its trade during the 17th century?
3. What was happening to the Mughal Empire by the 1740s?
4. Why was the Treaty of Allahabad a turning point in the history of the British in India?
5. How far had British rule in India spread by 1815?

Unit 1: The British Empire
Australia

On 26 August, 1768, the British government sent a naval captain called James Cook to explore the South Pacific Ocean on board a ship named the *Endeavour.*

Portrait of Captain James Cook

Part of Cook's mission was to claim for Britain a mysterious continent in the South Pacific Ocean which had been encountered by European sailors, but so far lay unexplored. It was known as *Terra Australis*, Latin for 'Southern land'.

Captain Cook grew up the son of a poor farm labourer in Yorkshire, and left home aged seventeen to work at sea. Cook joined the Royal Navy in 1755, and despite his poor background was quickly promoted through the ranks. Intelligent and hard-working, Cook taught himself Greek, geometry and astronomy – all subjects needed to be able to navigate at sea. By 1768, Cook had gained a reputation as the most able navigator in the Royal Navy.

From 1769 to 1770, Cook sailed around the two islands of New Zealand, and mapped its coastline. The *Endeavour* then continued west to the southeastern tip of Australia, where in April 1770 Cook anchored in a large bay. One member of his crew – an enthusiastic botanist called Joseph Banks – went onshore in search of new plant species. Banks found so many new specimens that Cook named their landing site 'Botany Bay'. The *Endeavour* then continued along the eastern shore of Australia, as Cook drew a detailed map of its coastline.

On 11 June, the *Endeavour* struck the Great Barrier Reef, and began to sink. The crew only managed to keep the ship afloat by plugging the hole with an old sail, and landing again on the Australian coast to carry out urgent repairs. On 13 September 1770, Cook claimed Australia for King George III, and the patched-up *Endeavour* returned to Britain. After three years at sea, Cook was welcomed home a national hero.

Settlement

On returning to Britain, Joseph Banks suggested to Parliament that they could solve the problem of Britain's overcrowded prisons by using Australia as a **penal colony**. Parliament agreed.

On 13 May 1788, the First Fleet of 11 convict ships reached Australia. Along with their prison guards, the ships carried 543 male convicts, and 189 female.

Contemporary illustration of the landing of convicts at Botany Bay

The convicts were settled in a cove north of Botany Bay, which was named Sydney after the Government Minister who had sanctioned the colony. Over the next 80 years, around 161 000 convicts were deported from Britain to work as prisoners in Australia.

Death of Captain Cook

In 1776, Cook embarked on his third Pacific voyage, and he landed with his crew on the island of Hawaii in January 1779. They were the first Europeans to visit Hawaii, and the islanders welcomed Cook as a god, throwing a lavish festival in his honour. But as the visitors outstayed their welcome, relations soured. During an argument over a stolen boat, Captain Cook was caught by the islanders and clubbed to death.

Convicts were usually sentenced to seven years of forced labour, often for crimes as minor as stealing chickens from a farm. However, those convicts who survived their sentence were able to start a new life in Australia. Former convicts were granted free land to farm, and many played an important role in the early life of the country.

Over the course of the 19th century, Australia was transformed from a penal colony into a prosperous outpost of the British Empire. Much of this wealth was due to the introduction of merino sheep from Spain, whose fine wool was highly sought after in Europe. What sugar was to Barbados, wool was to Australia. By 1821 there were 38 000 people, and 290 000 sheep on the island.

As the British settlers in Australia prospered, however, the indigenous population suffered terribly. Known as **Aboriginal Australians**, they were a nomadic hunter-gatherer people, who had inhabited Australia for at least 50 000 years. But just like the Native Americans, Aboriginal Australians were devastated by conflict with the Europeans, and diseases such as smallpox.

As British settlers claimed Aboriginal hunting lands, more Aboriginal Australians starved or died in long running battles with the colonists. The worst abuses occurred on the island of Tasmania, where British settlers hunted and systematically killed the native population until – in 1876 – there was not a single Aboriginal Australian left on the island.

Many in Britain were appalled by the fate of the Aboriginal Australians, and Parliament appointed an Aboriginal Protector to Australia in 1838. Despite this, it has been estimated that between 1788 and 1900, Australia's Aboriginal population decreased by 90 per cent.

Fact

Mary Reibey was convicted of horse stealing in Lancashire at the age of 13 in 1790, and transported as a convict to Australia. Having served her sentence, Reibey became a successful hotel-owner, moneylender, and businesswoman. By 1820, she had accumulated a fortune of £20 000.

Aboriginal Australians using traditional methods to catch fish

Check your understanding

1. How did James Cook rise to become a Captain in the Royal Navy?
2. What did Captain Cook achieve on his first voyage to the Pacific Ocean?
3. Who were the first British settlers in Australia?
4. What became the source of Australia's early wealth as a colony?
5. How did the British settlers treat the indigenous population in Australia?

Unit 1: The British Empire
Ruling the waves

British merchants needed the Royal Navy to protect them from foreign attacks, so that they could trade safely with Britain's overseas colonies.

As an island nation, Britain had long been proud of its navy. However, by the 1740s the Royal Navy was in a dire condition, and suffered a string of embarrassing defeats at the hands of the French and Spanish.

The man charged with reforming the Royal Navy was a battle-hardened **Admiral** called George Anson. Made **First Lord of the Admiralty** in 1751, Lord Anson introduced sweeping reforms. He took control of the marines from the army, giving the Royal Navy a crack force of soldiers who could fight both on land and at sea. He also introduced a uniform for naval officers, consisting of a blue coat and white breeches. And he greatly increased naval discipline. This new level of discipline was revealed in 1756, when Admiral Byng lost Britain's important Mediterranean colony of Minorca. Back in England, the 52-year-old Admiral was shot by firing squad.

George Anson, First Lord of the Admiralty who reformed the Royal Navy

Most importantly, Anson persuaded the government to invest in new, state of the art ships. Britain's enormous dockyards in Portsmouth, Plymouth, Deptford and Chatham employed thousands of men, building large 74-gun battleships for naval wars, and smaller 36-gun frigates for scouting and protecting merchant ships. The 104-gun HMS *Victory*, which was launched in 1765, took 6000 trees to build.

HMS *Victory*, today preserved as a museum in Portsmouth

Seven Years' War

The **Seven Years' War** began in 1756, and was the world's first truly global conflict. The war was mainly fought between Britain and France, but fighting spread across the world to their colonies. Battles were fought in North America, the Caribbean, Africa and India – where Robert Clive won his victory at Plassey in 1757 (see pages 8–9).

In 1759, Britain launched an attack on **Quebec**, the capital of the French possessions in North America (part of present-day Canada). With the help of the Royal Navy, 4600 troops under the leadership of General Wolfe sailed up the St Lawrence River towards Quebec at night. On 13 September, they took the city in a surprise attack. General Wolfe was killed, but his victory gave Britain almost complete control of North America.

> **Fact**
>
> Sailors who did not follow orders risked being flogged by the cat o' nine tails, a whip made of nine knotted leather cords, designed to cut the skin.

Later that year on 20 November, the Royal Navy defeated the French Navy off the coast of France at the Battle of **Quiberon Bay**. The French were planning to invade Britain, but the Royal Navy intercepted a fleet of 27 ships. Six French ships were destroyed, and one was captured.

The Royal Navy went on to capture Havana and Manila (in the Philippines) from the Spanish, and a number of French islands in the Caribbean. When the Treaty of Paris was signed with the French in 1763, Britain had expanded its power in India, taken French territories in North America and the Caribbean, and retained its power in the Mediterranean by keeping **Gibraltar** and Minorca.

The end of the Seven Years' War marked the beginning of Britain's global dominance, which would last 150 years. At the root of this dominance lay the Royal Navy. By 1800, the British had 285 major battleships in service around the world, more than the French, Spanish, Dutch and Danish fleets combined.

Life as a British seaman

The Royal Navy grew from around 12 000 men during the early 18th century, to 85 000 men in 1763, and 150 000 by 1815.

Naval ships could go for months without touching dry land, so it was impossible to eat fresh food. Seamen lived off a diet of meat preserved in salt, and dry biscuits which were often riddled with worms and insects. The lack of vitamin C in a sailor's diet meant many suffered from **scurvy**, a disease which caused their gums to rot, teeth to fall out, and bodies to become covered in ulcers. Scurvy killed far more seamen than active combat during the 18th century. Recruiting enough men to join the navy could be difficult, so **press gangs** visited towns and cities along the British coast and forced sailors to join.

However, service in the Royal Navy did hold some opportunities. When an enemy merchant ship was captured, the prize money would be shared out among the crew, and naval seamen liked to flaunt their wealth with colourful clothing and gold earrings. Royal Navy seamen were nicknamed 'Jack Tars'. Some would cover their arms in naval tattoos, a practice learned from the tribespeople Captain Cook encountered in Tahiti. And their drink of choice was rum. Made from Caribbean sugar, British sailors were entitled to a ration of half a pint of rum a day.

Contemporary Illustration of a British soldier being flogged with a cat o' nine tails.

Check your understanding

1. Why was the Royal Navy in need of reform after the 1740s?
2. What reforms did Lord Anson make to the Royal Navy from 1751?
3. In what parts of the world was the Seven Years' War fought?
4. Why did the end of the Seven Years' War mark the start of Britain's role as a global power?
5. Why did so many seamen in the Royal Navy die of scurvy?

Unit 1: The British Empire
Wealth and trade

As trade between Britain and its colonies developed and the volume of foreign **imports** increased, their prices dropped dramatically.

In 1620 smoking was a luxury confined to the upper classes, as a pound of tobacco cost 36 pennies. By the 1660s, a pound of tobacco cost just one penny. A doctor, Thomas Tryon, complained in 1691: "Now every plow-man has his pipe to himself."

Sugar became Britain's biggest import during the 18th century, growing from 20 million kg in 1650 to 400 million kg in 1820. At the end of the 18th century, an English writer estimated that workers in southern England were spending 11 per cent of their wages on sugar, treacle and tea.

The amount of tea imported from China by the East India Company increased from 1 million kg in 1720 to 14.5 million kg in 1790. Though tea is drunk on its own in China, the British took to combining it with milk and sugar, creating a national drink that persists to this day. Sugar was combined with spices from the Far East such as ginger, nutmeg and cinnamon to create dishes we now see as typically British: cakes, spiced buns and chutneys.

> **Fact**
>
> The wealthy took their tea in finely made white porcelain imported from China, which was prized for its thinness. This porcelain became known, unsurprisingly, as 'china'.
>
>

Colonial trade also changed how people dressed. At the beginning of the 18th century, a couple from a modest background would have dressed exclusively in linen and woollen cloth produced in Britain, often of dull colours. By the end of the 18th century, a woman could wear fine cotton textiles or Chinese silk, while her husband could wear a fashionable tricorn hat made from Canadian beaver fur. These clothes would have been noticeably more colourful, thanks to imported dyes such as indigo.

Mr and Mrs Andrews, painted by Thomas Gainsborough around 1750, wearing clothing made fashionable by Empire

Goods which had once been seen as luxuries had become necessities. To house these goods, the number of shops in Britain exploded from 50 000 in 1688 to 162 000 in 1759. Some historians claim that Britain became a **consumer society** for the first time during the 18th century.

Mercantilism

During this period, European countries did not trade freely with one another. They protected their own trade, and discouraged trade with their European rivals. This was a policy known as **mercantilism**.

A series of laws passed at the end of the 17th century called the Navigation Acts established how trade in the British Empire would function. All trade to and from British colonies had to be carried in British ships. Taxes known as **customs duties** were placed on imports from other European countries, to encourage trade with the Empire.

Mercantilism made Britain the centre of global trade. Goods from British colonies in America, Asia and the Pacific all had to pass through British ports before continuing their journey to other parts of Europe, allowing British merchants to make a tidy profit. By 1770, 85 per cent of tobacco that arrived in Britain was re-exported to other parts of the world, as was 94 per cent of coffee.

Painting of goods being unloaded at the West India Docks in London, 1840

Ports such as London, Bristol, Liverpool and Glasgow were Britain's fastest growing cities during this period. By the mid-18th century, 6000 merchant ships were coming in and out of these ports – twice the number of merchant ships in France.

British identity

The nation of Britain was only formed through the 1707 Act of Union, which united England and Scotland. During the years that followed, a British national identity began to form around Britain's role as a global power. The Scottish and Irish played a major role in building Britain's Empire. It has been estimated that three quarters of all British settlers in overseas colonies after 1700 came from either Scotland or Ireland, and half of those who served in the East India Company were Scottish.

The female figure of **Britannia**, with her Union Jack shield, came to symbolise the growing **patriotism** in Britain. In 1744, the first version of Britain's national anthem, 'God Save the King', was published. Politicians who appealed to the empire and patriotism could ensure great support, such as William Pitt who became Prime Minister during the Seven Years' War. Pitt knew the value of empire: his own family fortune came from his grandfather, the famous nabob 'Diamond Pitt', trading in India (see page 8).

Image of Britannia, on the reverse of the old 50p coin

In 1740, a song which was to become linked with the British Empire for generations was performed for the first time. Its chorus went:

"Rule Britannia! Rule the waves:
Britons never will be slaves."

These lyrics pointed to the dark heart of the British Empire. As you will learn in the next chapter, Britain's buoyant trade in consumer goods was built on African slavery.

Check your understanding

1. What consumer goods became widely available in Britain during the 18th century?
2. How did colonial trade change the way that people dressed?
3. How did the policy of mercantilism encourage trade with Britain's colonies?
4. What effect did colonial trade have on cities in Britain?
5. How did a new British national identity emerge during the 18th century?

Unit 1: The British Empire
Knowledge organiser

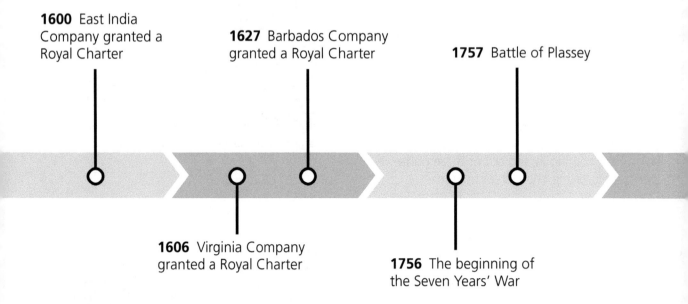

1600 East India Company granted a Royal Charter

1627 Barbados Company granted a Royal Charter

1757 Battle of Plassey

1606 Virginia Company granted a Royal Charter

1756 The beginning of the Seven Years' War

Key vocabulary

Aboriginal Australians Nomadic hunter-gatherer population native to Australia and nearby islands

Admiral Highest ranking naval officer, usually in command of a fleet

Barbados Caribbean island, and one of England's firstmajorsugar -producing colonies

Battle of Plassey Key victory for Clive and the East India Company against the *nawab* of Bengal

Bengal Wealthy province in northeast India, where the British built their factory called Calcutta

Britannia A female figur e, used to symbolise Britain and popular during the British Empire

Consumer society A society where people can afford to buy non-essential 'consumer' goods

Customs duties Taxes placed by a government on goods imported from foreign countries

East India Company Private company formed in 1600 with rights to trade between India and England

Endeavour The ship that Captain Cook sailed on his firstvoyagetoAustralia

Exports Goods or services sold to other countries

Factories (colonial) Coastal trading posts where merchants can do business in foreign lands

First Lord of the Admiralty Head of the Royal Navy

Gibraltar British colony at the southern tip of Spain, gained in 1713

Imports Goods or services brought in from other countries

Indigenous Originating in a particular place

Mayflower Ship that carried the first settlers to New England in 1620

Mercantilism The economic practice of discouraging trade with rival nations

Mughals Dynasty originally from Central Asia that ruled much of India from the 16th to 19th century

Nawab Prince granted a province of India to rule on behalf of the Mughal Emperor

Patriotism Showing strong support for your own country

Penal colony A remote settlement used to exile convicted criminals from the general population

1759 (September) Britain wins the Battle of Quebec

1765 Treaty of Allahabad

1788 The First Fleet of 11 convict ships reaches Australia

1763 The Treaty of Paris ends the Seven Years' War

1770 Captain Cook claims Australia for Britain

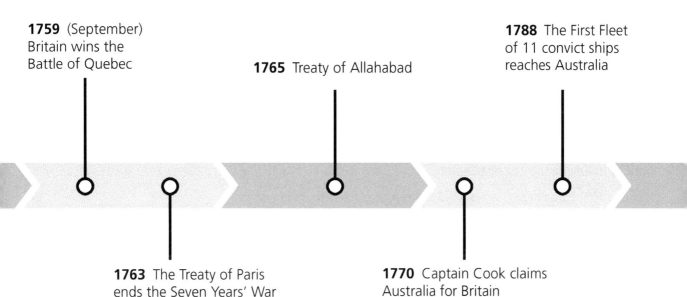

Key vocabulary

Pilgrim Fathers The first settlers in New England, known for their religious Puritanism

Press gangs Groups who would travel Britain forcing men to enlist in the Army or Navy

Quebec Capital of French possessions in America, now a city in present day Canada

Quiberon Bay Battle in which the British defeated the French navy, preventing invasion

Scurvy Disease caused by a lack of vitamin C, which killed many sailors in the Royal Navy

Seven Years' War Global conflict, which saw Britain emerge as a dominant world power

Thirteen colonies The original British settlements along the east coast of North America

Treaty of Allahabad Treaty granting government of Bengal province to the East India Company

Virginia The first English colony in North America, named after Elizabeth I

Key people

General Wolfe British army officer who led the capture of Quebec in 1759

George Anson First Lord of the Admiralty who introduced sweeping reforms to the Royal Navy

James Cook British explorer and navigator who mapped Australia's eastern coastline

Joseph Banks Botanist on board the *Endeavour* who studied Australia's plants and wildlife

Robert Clive Officer in the East India Company who became Governor of Bengal Province

Thomas Pitt British merchant in India, made his fortune selling the world's largest diamond

William Pitt British politician, made Prime Minister during the Seven Years' War

Unit 2: The Americas
American Revolution

By the late 18th century, the thirteen colonies had a population of 2.4 million people. They were growing rapidly in size, wealth and importance.

At first, Britain gave the American colonies a large degree of freedom to govern themselves. Following the hugely expensive Seven Years' War, however, the British government wanted to exert more control. After all, they reasoned, the campaign to take Canada from the French had been fought to ensure the colonists' safety.

So, in 1765, Parliament passed the **Stamp Act**. It ruled that American colonists had to buy special paper from the British government, with a particular 'stamp', in order to print legal documents, advertisements, newspapers, and even playing cards.

The colonists were furious, and protested against the tax. Violent demonstrations took place in **Boston**, where an angry mob destroyed the house of the lieutenant-governor of Massachusetts. It soon became clear that the stamp duty would be impossible to collect, as the colonists would simply refuse to pay it.

In 1766, Parliament repealed the Stamp Act. But they also declared that they retained "full power and authority to make laws…to bind the colonies and people of America". The following year, Parliament imposed new customs duties on the American colonies on imports such as tea, glass and paper, and took measures to clamp down on smuggling. Once again, the colonists refused to pay these duties, and most of them were repealed over the following years.

The phrase that came to define the colonists' objection to British rule was "no taxation without **representation**". Each of the thirteen colonies had an elected Colonial Assembly, and the colonists were happy paying tax to them, as they were their chosen representatives. But the colonists had no representatives in the British Parliament, so Parliament – they believed – had no right to tax them.

Trouble in Boston

The strongest opposition to British rule in America could be found in Boston, Massachusetts. In 1768 the British stationed troops in Boston, and the atmosphere in the city grew tense. In March 1770, an angry demonstration led British soldiers to open fire on the crowd, and five Boston citizens were killed. News quickly spread to other colonies of the 'Boston Massacre', and Britain was accused of tyranny.

Engraving of the 1770 Boston Massacre by Paul Revere

In 1773, Parliament passed the Tea Act, enforcing the East India Company's **monopoly** to sell tea to the American colonies. When a shipment of East India tea arrived in Boston later that year, a group of Bostonians dressed as Native Americans boarded the ship, and tipped 342 boxes into Boston Harbour (enough to brew 18 million cups of tea!). This protest became known as the Boston Tea Party.

Print depicting the 1773 Boston Tea Party, produced in 1846

Britain's king at the time was George III. He was furious at the behaviour of the rebellious colonists, and insisted that they should be put in their place. In 1774, a series of laws were passed stationing 4000 troops in Boston, stripping Massachusetts of its self-governance, and placing the colony under the direct rule of a new Royal Governor from the British army. Colonists began splitting into 'rebels' who opposed British rule in the colonies, and **loyalists** who remained loyal to the king.

On 19 April, 1775, a detachment of British troops marched from Boston to find weapons that had been stockpiled by rebels in a nearby town. At a village called Lexington, the British troops were stopped by a rebel militia, and the two sides fired on each other. The American Revolution had begun. As the American poet Ralph Waldo Emerson later wrote, it was a "shot heard around the world".

Independence

Thomas Jefferson, principal author of the Declaration of Independence

In 1774, delegates from 12 out of the 13 colonies met in Philadelphia, America's largest city, for the first **Continental Congress**. This gathering saw the colonies unite in opposition to British rule for the first time. Colonists who had previously seen themselves as Virginians, Pennsylvanians or New Englanders started to call themselves Americans.

At first, the rebels were fighting for the right not to be taxed by Parliament. But as full-scale war became a reality, some colonists began to argue that their future lay in separation from Great Britain. At the second meeting of the Continental Congress in July 1776, the delegates voted for complete independence from Britain. Thomas Jefferson, a well-read lawyer and **plantation** owner from Virginia, was chosen to write the formal **Declaration of Independence**. It was approved on 4 July 1776.

According to the Declaration, the thirteen colonies were to become independent states, governed as part of a new country called the United States of America. But it would take six more years of fighting to make this declaration a reality.

Fact
....
To this day, the Americans celebrate Independence Day every 4 July as the birth of their nation.

Check your understanding

1. How did British government of the thirteen colonies change following the Seven Years' War?

2. Why did the American colonists adopt the slogan "no taxation without representation"?

3. How did the British respond to the growing unrest in Boston in 1774?

4. When did the American Revolution begin?

5. What was the American Declaration of Independence?

Unit 2: The Americas
American War of Independence

In June 1776, an army of 32 000 British troops under the command of General Howe arrived to take New York from the American rebels.

General Howe's army was made up of battle-hardened British and German soldiers, and was supported by the strongest navy in the world. In contrast, the American army consisted almost entirely of untrained volunteers.

The British campaign started well. An American force attempted to capture Quebec in December 1775 and bring the Canadians onto their side, but failed. Meanwhile in August 1776, the British took the vital port city of New York, which would remain as their base for the rest of the war. The following year, General Howe took the rebel capital of Philadelphia, forcing the Continental Congress to flee.

However, as the war dragged on the British found it difficult to sustain their early success. British strategy was directed from 3000 miles away in London. This meant orders could take up to three months to cross the Atlantic, and orders took another three months to return. In addition, the British army was hampered by the sheer size and wildness of the thirteen colonies, which covered an area six times that of Great Britain.

American successes

In June 1775, Congress created a **Continental Army** to replace the individual state militias. Congress chose a Virginian wheat farmer called George Washington to be the Commander-in-Chief. Standing at 6'2", Washington was a stern but inspiring presence. His only military experience had been in fighting for the British during the Seven Years' War. But Washington made up for this lack of experience with sheer hard work, turning the Continental Army from a band of rebels into a professional fighting force.

George Washington, Commander-in-Chief of the Continental Army during the War of Independence

The Continental Army's turning point came in 1777. A British force under the command of General Burgoyne left Canada in June, and planned to march south towards New York, trapping the Continental Army. However, Burgoyne did not realise how difficult it would be to travel with full supplies and artillery through the thick forests of North America. There was only one basic road, which rebel soldiers had repeatedly blocked by cutting down trees.

After five months, 1300 of Burgoyne's army had been killed, wounded or captured. On 17 October, the Continental Army surrounded his remaining force of around 6000 men at a town called **Saratoga**, located 160 miles north of New York. Burgoyne and his entire army were forced to surrender, and taken prisoner.

> ## Fact
>
> At the beginning of the war, British troops sang a song called Yankee Doodle to mock the disorganised 'Yankee' rebels. This became a source of pride for the Americans, who began referring to themselves as 'Yankees'.

Victory

At the start of the war, Congress sent Benjamin Franklin, a famous scientist and writer from Philadelphia, to be their ambassador in France. When Franklin brought the news of the American victory at Saratoga to the French king, France agreed to join the war on America's side. France provided Washington's army with crucial support, including a navy of 24 battleships.

Even though British victory now seemed impossible, George III and his ministers refused to give in. In 1780, the British changed their focus to the southern colonies, where a British officer called Lord Cornwallis fought a successful campaign.

In response, Washington abandoned his attempts to capture New York, and took his army on a daring march south. Washington trapped Cornwallis's army on the Virginian coast at Yorktown, and a blockade by the French navy prevented any British chances of escape. On 17 October, 1781, Cornwallis surrendered, and 7500 British troops were taken prisoner.

The British Parliament voted to end the war in April 1782, and the last British troops left New York the following year. The most powerful empire in the world had been brought to its knees by a band of rebel colonists. George III was distraught, and the rest of the world looked on in disbelief.

Print depicting the surrender of Lord Cornwallis to the American army at Yorktown

Forging a nation

The men who steered America towards independence and victory, such as Thomas Jefferson, Benjamin Franklin and George Washington, became known as America's **Founding Fathers**. Their next job was to decide how their new nation should be governed.

James Madison, the son of a Virginia plantation owner, was given the task of writing a series of laws establishing how politics in the United States would function. Known as the United States **Constitution**, it was approved in June 1788. The Constitution promised liberty to all American people, but one group was noticeably missing from this vision: 700 000 African–American slaves.

The Capitol Building in Washington D.C., where the Unites States Congress still meets today

In 1789, George Washington was made the first President of the United States. The following year, Congress approved the construction of a new capital city, named 'Washington' in honour of America's first President.

Check your understanding

1. What early successes did the British achieve during the War of Independence?
2. Why did General Burgoyne's campaign in 1777 fail?
3. What role did Benjamin Franklin play during the War of Independence?
4. What events finally led to American victory in the War of Independence?
5. How did the Founding Fathers create a new nation following the War?

Unit 2: The Americas
Transatlantic slave trade

Between the 16th and the 19th centuries, European merchants transported an estimated 12.5 million Africans across the Atlantic to work in slavery in the Americas.

By the mid-17th century, the growing British sugar plantations of the **Caribbean** needed workers. The native population could not do the work as so many of them had been killed by European diseases. Few British people were willing to work in the Caribbean, once they were aware of the conditions and risk of death.

The answer lay in transporting slaves from Africa. This practice had already been developed by Spain and Portugal, whose ships had long transported Africans to their South American colonies. In 1672, Charles II granted a charter for the **Royal African Company** to trade with West Africa, but soon the trade was opened up to independent British merchants.

Cape Coast Castle in present day Ghana. Once used by the British as a factory to house enslaved Africans

The **transatlantic** journey formed part of a lucrative **triangular trade**. Merchants left Britain for West Africa with a cargo of manufactured goods, such as Indian textiles, alcohol, cooking pots, and guns. These goods were then sold in Africa in exchange for slaves. Merchants carried the African slaves across the Atlantic on the **middle passage** to the Americas, where they sold them for raw goods such as sugar and tobacco. Finally, the merchants transported these raw goods from America back to Britain, where they sold them for a significant profit on their initial investment.

Middle passage

The transatlantic slave trade began in Africa, where African traders captured and enslaved members of rival African kingdoms. Captives were joined at the neck by **shackles**, and marched in lines known as **coffles** towards the coast. Here, captives were imprisoned in European fortresses known as factories, such as Britain's Cape Coast Castle in present-day Ghana.

When the slave ship arrived, captives were marched on board and forced below deck, where they were stacked lengthways on wooden shelves and kept in place with chains. Slaves developed open wounds as their arms and legs rubbed against their shackles, and sores where their naked bodies rested on the shelves.

Unable to move, the slaves became surrounded by vomit, excrement and urine. When this combined with the stifling heat, diseases such as dysentery spread rapidly. The stench was so noxious that many claimed you could smell a slave ship at sea before you could see it. If the weather was calm,

Illustration of the *Brookes* slave ship from 1788, showing the conditions in which slaves were kept

the slaves were taken up on deck once a day to exercise. Slaves were kept in these horrific conditions for two to three months during the middle passage, and many died before reaching the Americas. Their bodies were simply thrown overboard.

During the early days of the slave trade, as many as one in four slaves died before making it to America. It has been estimated that between 1640 and 1807, British merchants transported 3.1 million slaves across the Atlantic, 2.7 million of whom survived

Human trade

Having crossed the Atlantic, merchants could sell a slave in the Americas for up to eight times the price they paid in Africa. At first, Britain's Caribbean islands were the main marketplaces. But as the 18th century progressed, slaves were increasingly sold to work in Britain's North American colonies such as Virginia, Georgia and the Carolinas.

The wealth of British cities such as Liverpool and Bristol came to depend on the slave trade. Rich slave owners would return to Britain with their fortunes, and built magnificent country houses, libraries for Oxford colleges, and art collections which now sit in our national galleries. As one slave trader told Parliament in 1772, the slave trade "[is] the foundation of our commerce, the support of our colonies, the life of our navigation, and first cause of our national industry and riches".

Though slavery had existed throughout human history, nothing had ever been as systematic as the transatlantic slave trade. As the 18th century came to an end, British opponents of this inhumane trade were making their voices heard.

Fact

Some captured Africans believed the European slave traders were cannibals, and intended to eat them. They believed that the red wine drunk by the Europeans was the blood of fellow captives.

Olaudah Equiano

Equiano was a slave on the Caribbean island of Montserrat who bought his own freedom in 1766. He moved to London in 1767, married an Englishwoman called Susanna, and became a prominent anti-slavery campaigner.

In 1789, Equiano published his autobiography. He recalled being born in present-day Nigeria, and sold into slavery at the age of 11. Equiano described the horrors of the Middle Passage in vivid detail, writing: "The shrieks of the women, and the groans of the dying, rendered the whole scene of horror almost inconceivable". However, some historians have argued Equiano was actually born into slavery in America.

Check your understanding
1. Why did the British begin transporting slaves across the Atlantic?
2. Why was the triangular trade so lucrative?
3. Why did so many African slaves die during the Middle Passage?
4. How many slaves, in total, are British traders estimated to have transported?
5. How did Britain benefit from the slave trade?

Life as a slave

Once African slaves finished their journey across the Atlantic Ocean, their suffering was far from over.

Newly arrived slaves were auctioned in large markets, where customers were allowed to inspect the slaves before bidding. To make the slaves appear healthy, slave traders would have them washed, shaved, and rubbed with palm oil. Any sores or wounds that the slaves had developed during the middle passage were disguised with hot tar.

The slaves then had to become accustomed to the tropical climate and develop immunity to local diseases, a process known as 'seasoning'. This was the most dangerous period for new arrivals, and many would die within their first year.

Plantation owners knew that the more memories a slave kept of life in Africa, the more likely they were to rebel. For this reason, slaves from different African kingdoms were grouped together so that they did not share a common language, and families were deliberately split up. Owners gave their slaves new names, and some owners branded their initials onto the slaves' skin.

19th-century illustration of slaves harvesting sugar cane in the Caribbean

Working as a slave

Working in Caribbean sugar cane plantations was exhausting. The tough cane had to be cut and transported to a mill, where it would be crushed to release the sugar juice. The juice was then boiled in vats, leaving a residue of solid sugar. Slaves were organised to work in 'gangs', and overseen by a slave driver. Armed with a whip, the slave driver provided a constant threat of violence to ensure that the slaves kept working.

Work on the rice fields of North and South Carolina was equally tough, but the tobacco plantations of Virginia tended to be less demanding. Slaves were also put to work building roads, clearing fields, mining, and felling timber. One of the worst jobs was working in the salt ponds of the Turks and Caicos Islands, where standing for long hours in the salt water caused blisters and boils to spread across slaves' legs.

A small minority of slaves were taken into the plantation owner's house, where they worked as cooks, servants or cleaners. Some were given a basic education, so they could work as a clerk or secretary. Being a house slave meant a more comfortable existence, though female house slaves were at risk of being sexually exploited by their owners.

The life expectancy for a slave was short, perhaps eight to ten years. In the Caribbean, where working conditions were the hardest, the slave population was still only 300 000 in 1750, despite a total of 800 000 Africans having been shipped to the islands. In the North American colonies, slaves survived long enough and had enough children for their population steadily to increase.

African culture

Despite the attempts to remove slaves' memories of home, African traditions combined with life in the colonies to form a distinctive culture. This encompassed food, language, music and religion. In the American South, the banjo has its roots in Africa, as does the pirogue boat used to navigate the marshes of Louisiana.

Resistance

Some slaves escaped their plantations and fled inland to the forests and mountains, where they established settlements for runaway slaves. Known as **Maroons**, they would raid their former plantations, before disappearing back into the forest.

During the 1730s, the British Army waged a war against the Maroons in Jamaica. Hidden deep in the forest, the Maroons proved impossible to track down and defeat, so a truce was agreed in 1739. The British granted the Maroons freedom and their own land, in return for stopping their raids and returning any newly escaped slaves to their owners. Violent uprisings frequently took place in Barbados and other Caribbean islands.

Other slaves engaged in more minor forms of resistance, such as working slowly, setting fire to crops, or damaging plantation machinery. Some slaves committed suicide in the desperate belief that death might finally return them to Africa.

In response, slave owners used extreme violence to discourage slaves from rebelling, and to keep them working hard. Slaves caught resisting their owners would be whipped, imprisoned, starved and tortured. Some slaves would be placed in spiked shackles to stop them from running, others placed in iron muzzles to stop them from speaking and eating. One slave owner in Jamaica recorded whipping his slaves, and then rubbing lime, salt, and pepper into the open wounds. Slave labour depended upon violence, intimidation and fear.

Fact

The most successful rebellion by enslaved Africans took place in the French colony of Saint Domingue in 1791. Led by an inspiring former slave called Toussaint L'Ouverture, the slaves rose up against their slave-owners and won their freedom in 1793. After a long war with France, Saint Domingue's former slaves established Haiti, the first black-led nation in the Caribbean, in 1804.

Toussaint L'Ouverture, leader of the Haitian Revolution against French rule

Check your understanding
1. What did slave traders do to make their African slaves appear healthy at auction?
2. What measures did slave owners take to make slaves forget about their lives in Africa?
3. How did the jobs undertaken by slaves vary?
4. Why did the British grant Jamaican Maroons their own land in 1739?
5. How did slaves resist and rebel against their captivity?

Unit 2: The Americas
Abolition

From the 1780s, a growing number of British people started to campaign for the abolition of the slave trade. They were known as **abolitionists.**

One of the most important British abolitionists was an **evangelical** Christian called Thomas Clarkson. In 1787, Clarkson helped form the **Society for the Abolition of the Slave Trade**. He hoped that by increasing awareness amongst British people about the reality of slavery, the public would place enough pressure on Parliament to outlaw the trade.

Abolitionist campaign

Clarkson led the abolitionist campaign with enormous energy. He claimed to have ridden 35 000 miles in seven years, travelling the country to build support. In particular, Clarkson visited British ports, where he collected objects used by slave traders, such as shackles, whips and **branding** irons. Clarkson used these objects to shock his audiences in public talks.

In 1792, the Society organised for 519 **petitions** to be sent to Parliament asking for an end to the slave trade, the largest number of petitions ever submitted on a single issue. Abolitionists also organised a **boycott** of sugar from the **West Indies**, in which an estimated 300 000 people took part. They published a flood of books and pamphlets describing the horrors of the slave trade in vivid detail. The most powerful books were written by former slaves themselves, such as Olaudah Equiano (see page 23) and, during in the 19th century, Mary Prince.

Josiah Wedgewood, a wealthy industrialist, produced a distinctive badge for the Society, so that members of the public could show their support for abolition. The motto on the badge emphasised one of the abolitionists' key arguments: that enslaved Africans should be treated like fellow human beings. It asked, "Am I not a man and a brother?"

Abolition gained widespread public support in Britain, but supporters of slavery fought back. Plantation owners argued that if Parliament outlawed slavery in British colonies, then British sugar exports would become too expensive. They would then be unable to compete with sugar still produced by slaves in colonies such as Cuba or Brazil.

Political success

The abolitionist cause gained important support in Parliament from another evangelical Christian, William Wilberforce. He repeatedly proposed Bills in Parliament to abolish the slave trade, but they struggled to gain support – especially in the House of Lords.

Portrait of Thomas Clarkson, prominent abolitionist and anti-slavery campaigner

The Abolitionists' badge, designed by Josiah Wedgewood

In 1806, Britain gained a new Prime Minister called Lord Grenville, who strongly supported abolition. Grenville introduced a new Bill to Parliament in January 1807. At 4 am on 24 February 1807, after a ten-hour debate in the House of Commons, the Slave Trade Act was passed by 283 votes to 16.

However, this Act only outlawed the slave trade. Abolitionists had to campaign for 26 more years to achieve the outright abolition of slavery. In 1828, the abolitionists organised for a new petition to be sent to Parliament, which was signed by one and a half million British people. This time, the campaign spread to the West Indies itself, where slaves received news about the campaign against slavery in Britain. Convinced their owners were refusing them their freedom, slaves organised large-scale rebellions in Barbados in 1816, and Jamaica in 1832.

Finally, in August 1833, Parliament passed the Slavery Abolition Act. This law made slavery illegal across the British Empire. One month before Parliament passed the Act, William Wilberforce – who had dedicated his life to this cause – died aged 73.

Portrait of William Wilberforce, the most significant abolitionist in Parliament

International pressure

Having become one of the first European nations to abolish slavery, Britain began a long campaign to persuade other nations to do the same. Britain encouraged European governments to sign international treaties, promising to stop the slave trade. These treaties were not always followed, so Britain sent the Royal Navy to patrol the West African coast.

Between 1807 and 1860, the Royal Navy intercepted more than 1500 slave ships, and freed 150 000 captured Africans. As the 19th century progressed, other nations followed Britain's lead. France abolished slavery in 1848, Holland in 1861, and America – following a fierce civil war – in 1865.

> **Fact**
>
> Following the Slavery Abolition Act, the British government paid compensation to slave owners for their loss of property, worth a total of £20 million. No compensation was paid to former slaves.

Black Britons

Some estimate that by the late 1700s, there were 10 000 black people living in Britain as free citizens. This group played a central role in the campaign for abolition.

One former slave called Ignatius Sancho was encouraged to read and write by his employer, the Duke of Montagu. Sancho became a published author, and was friends with some of the most famous actors, writers and artists of the period. Sancho is also believed to be the first black man to have participated in a British election, placing his vote in 1774.

Ignatius Sancho, a popular and well known figure in Georgian London

> ### Check your understanding
> **1.** What roles did Thomas Clarkson and William Wilberforce play in the abolitionist movement?
> **2.** What methods did abolitionists use to raise awareness about slavery?
> **3.** When was slavery abolished in the British Empire?
> **4.** What role did Britain play in encouraging the end of slavery worldwide?
> **5.** How large was Britain's black population during this period?

Unit 2: The Americas
Knowledge organiser

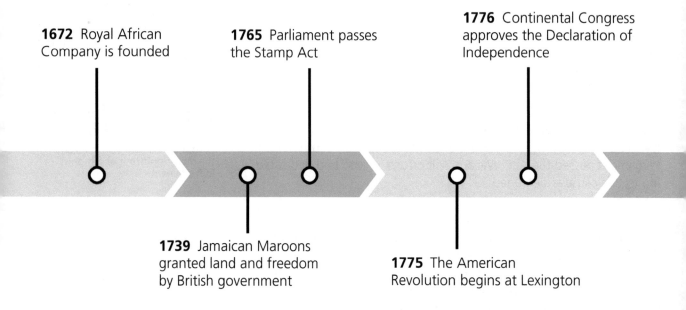

1672 Royal African Company is founded

1765 Parliament passes the Stamp Act

1776 Continental Congress approves the Declaration of Independence

1739 Jamaican Maroons granted land and freedom by British government

1775 The American Revolution begins at Lexington

Key vocabulary

Abolitionist Someone involved in the public campaign to end slavery or the slave trade

Boston City in Massachusetts, with strong opposition to British rule during the American Revolution

Boycott Organised refusal to purchase a particular product as an act of political or moral protest

Branding To mark a person or an animal with a hot iron, for ease of identification

Caribbean Sea to the east of Central America, containing many tropical islands

Coffle A line of slaves joined at the neck by shackles, leaving their legs free to walk

Constitution Series of laws establishing how a nation's political system functions

Continental Army Armed force representing all thirteen colonies, formed by Congress in 1775

Continental Congress Meeting of delegates from thirteen colonies that formed the United States

Declaration of Independence Formal statement which created the United States of America

Evangelical A Christian movement which seeks to save people's souls by spreading God's word

Founding Fathers Name given to the key figures in the creation of the United States of America

Loyalist Colonists who sided with Britain and the King during the American Revolution

Maroon An escaped African slave in the Caribbean

Middle passage Journey undertaken by slave ships from West Africa to the Americas by sea

Monopoly A company having exclusive control to trade in a particularly area

Petition A formal written request, often for a political cause, signed by many people

Plantation A large estate, on which crops such as coffee, sugar and tobacco are grown

Representation Political principle where elected officials serve the views of their citizens

Royal African Company Group founded by Charles II to trade with the West coast of Africa

Saratoga Site of a 1777 battle, and a key turning point in the War of Independence

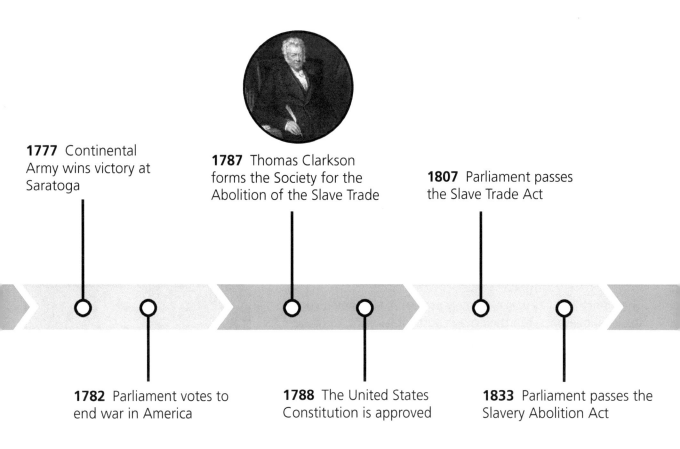

1777 Continental Army wins victory at Saratoga

1787 Thomas Clarkson forms the Society for the Abolition of the Slave Trade

1807 Parliament passes the Slave Trade Act

1782 Parliament votes to end war in America

1788 The United States Constitution is approved

1833 Parliament passes the Slavery Abolition Act

Key vocabulary

Shackles Iron chains used to fasten together the legs or hands of a slave or prisoner

Society for the Abolition of the Slave Trade Group formed in 1787 to campaign for an end to the slave trade

Stamp Act Controversial 1765 law which taxed legal and other documents in the American colonies

Transatlantic Going across the Atlantic Ocean

Triangular trade A trade system importing and exporting goods to and from three destinations

West Indies A region of tropical island nations in the Caribbean Sea and North Atlantic Ocean

Key people

Benjamin Franklin American writer and scientist, and Ambassador to France during the War of Independence

General Howe Commander of the British forces during the War of Independence

George III Hanoverian King of England from 1760 to 1820

George Washington Commander-in-chief of American forces during the War of Independence

Ignatius Sancho Well known 18th century black Briton, and the first to vote in an election

Olaudah Equiano Freed slave who lived in London as a prominent anti-slavery campaigner

Thomas Clarkson Leading campaigner against slavery and the slave trade

Thomas Jefferson Virginia plantation owner, and author of the Declaration of Independence

William Wilberforce The leading campaigner against slavery in the House of Commons

Unit 3: The French Revolution
The Ancien Régime

At the beginning of the 18th century, France was the most powerful country in Europe, but aspects of French politics and society had changed little since the times of feudalism.

For this reason French politics and society were known as the **Ancien Régime**. The king was an absolutist monarch, who ruled France from his magnificent palace of **Versailles**. From 1774, France's king was the childish and indecisive Louis XVI.

The French nobility was extremely powerful. Noblemen could tax local peasants, run their own courts of law, and demand unpaid labour for the upkeep of their estates. Out of a total population of 26 million people, the nobility numbered no more than 350 000, yet they owned one quarter of the land in France. Almost all senior members of the clergy, army officers, and government ministers in France came from the nobility.

France's Catholic Church had 100 000 clergymen, and owned a tenth of the land. Members of the clergy did not have to pay any tax, and had considerable power over French culture and education.

At the bottom of French society was the peasantry, who made up around 75 percent of the population. Peasants had the least money, but they were expected to pay the most taxes. Between one third and one half of a peasant's annual income was spent paying dues to the local landlord, a tithe to the Catholic Church, and other taxes to the French government. Many peasants lived in crushing poverty.

Portrait of the French King Louis XVI

Financial crisis

During the American Revolution, France sent troops and battleships to help General Washington's army defeat France's old enemy Britain (see pages 20–21). Though an important victory, the war left France with an enormous national debt.

Louis XVI knew that to pay off this debt, he had to reform France's taxation system. A series of finance ministers tried to pass reforms making the aristocracy pay more tax, but none of them succeeded.

By 1788, France was in crisis. A cold winter and a dry summer led to a poor harvest, which caused the price of bread to rise, and many peasants were left starving. Some members of France's growing middle class, known as the *bourgeoisie*, were calling for more **radical** reforms to government and taxation. Unable to pay the enormous interest on its debt, France was on the verge of bankruptcy.

Cartoon illustrating a French peasant holding up a priest and a nobleman, published in 1789

Revolution

In desperation, Louis XVI agreed to call the **Estates-General**. The Estates-General was a meeting of France's three 'estates'. The First Estate was the clergy, the Second was the aristocracy, and the Third came from the rest of French society – mostly wealthy members of the bourgeoisie. Previous French kings had used the Estates-General to approve government reforms, and Louis XVI wanted them to approve his new taxes.

Painting of the storming of the Bastille by an anonymous artist

The Estates-General met on 5 May 1789 in the Palace of Versailles. It was attended by 291 nobles, 300 members of the clergy, and 610 members of the Third Estate.

This was the first time the Estates-General had met since 1614, and there were long running disagreements about whether the Third Estate should have the power to out vote the First and Second Estates. Members of the Third Estate were angered by their treatment, but they knew they had the support of most of France. So, on 13 June the Third Estate broke away from the Estates-General, and formed a new body called the **National Assembly**.

Rumours then began to spread through Paris that Louis XVI planned to shut down the National Assembly, with the help of 20 000 French soldiers and foreign mercenaries who had been stationed in the city. The people of Paris were becoming increasingly angry. When Louis XVI's popular finance minister resigned, it was the last straw for the people of Paris.

On 14 July, a furious mob of Parisians stormed an army barracks, and seized 28 000 muskets. Soldiers from the French army began to desert their posts and join the mob. As it grew, the mob moved on to a large medieval fortress in the centre of Paris called the **Bastille**, where gunpowder and ammunition were kept. The mob stormed the Bastille, killed its governor, and placed his head on a spike.

On hearing of the storming of the Bastille, Louis XVI was advised not to suppress the rebellion with his army, as the troops were unlikely to follow his orders. It was clear that Louis XVI had lost control of his own country. The French Revolution had begun.

Fact

On arriving in Versailles, Louis XVI received the First and Second Estates in his magnificent Hall of Mirrors, but members of the Third Estate were not invited. While the Second Estate was permitted to wear satin suits, silver waistcoats, and silk cloaks, the Third Estate had to wear plain black coats.

Check your understanding

1. What powers did French noblemen have as part of the Ancien Régime?
2. Which group within French society was expected to pay the most taxes?
3. Why was France in crisis by 1788?
4. What was the Estates-General?
5. What event is said to have marked the beginning of the French Revolution?

Execution and terror

Two days after the storming of the Bastille, Louis XVI showed his support for the revolution by wearing a hat with a **revolutionary cockade.**

The cockade had three colours: red and blue, which were the traditional colours of Paris; and white, which was the colour of the French royal family. In 1790, these three colours were used as a new flag for post-revolutionary France – the Tricolour.

The National Assembly now had authority over France. The Assembly began to write a new constitution, which would protect the rights of the people and limit the powers of the king. On 5 August, the Assembly abolished feudalism, freeing France's peasantry from their obligations to the nobility. On 26 August, the Assembly passed the **Declaration of the Rights of Man**. This remarkable document promised representative government, freedom of speech, and equality before the law for all French citizens. As Revolution continued, its rallying cry became 'Liberty! Equality! Fraternity!'.

Few knew what Louis XVI thought about these changes. Sometimes he appeared supportive, and at other times he appeared opposed. On 6 October Louis and his family were taken from Versailles, and imprisoned in a royal palace in central Paris.

Engraving from 1794, depicting a French soldier and a sans-culottes

Polarisation

There was broad support in France for the reforms of the National Assembly, but this did not last long. France's population became increasingly **polarised** between those who wanted to see more radical change, and those who thought the revolution was going too far.

The National Assembly needed to raise money to pay for its reforms. In November 1789 it confiscated all land belonging to the Catholic Church. More anti-Catholic reforms followed, leading the Pope to condemn the Assembly in March 1791. Many French Catholics, who had supported the Revolution, now turned against it.

In June 1791, Louis XVI and his family escaped from their palace in disguise. Louis left a letter addressed 'to the French people' denouncing the Revolution, and attacking the National Assembly. But the royal family were caught later that night in a town called Varennes, and returned to Paris.

The 'flight to Varennes' was a critical mistake for Louis XVI. The revolutionaries lost all trust in their king, and hatred for his Austrian wife Marie Antoinette grew even more intense. This distrust was heightened when Marie Antoinette's brother, the Austrian Emperor, began preparations to invade France and restore Louis XVI's absolutist rule. In June 1792, France declared war on Austria and **Prussia**.

> ### Fact
>
> Within the Assembly, radicals tended to sit on the left of the chair, and defenders of the king sat on the right, giving birth to the modern terms 'left wing' and 'right wing'.

Hundreds of thousands of Frenchmen volunteered to join the French Revolutionary Army, and defend their Revolution against foreign invasion.

Parisian revolutionaries from the lower classes were known as **sans-culottes**. They refused to wear the 'culottes' (silk breeches) which were worn by members of the aristocracy and bourgeoisie. On 10 August 1792, the sans-culottes broke into the royal palace. They massacred 600 of the King's Swiss Guard, and placed the royal family under arrest. In September 1792, the monarchy was abolished and France became a republic. After a short trial, Louis XVI was executed on 25 January 1793. His wife, Marie Antoinette, was executed the following year.

Terror

Following the execution of Louis XVI, France spiralled into chaos. The Revolutionary Army was fighting to protect its borders against Prussia, Austria and Britain. But it was also fighting a civil war against counter-revolutionaries inside France. Across the country, anti-Catholic revolutionaries closed down churches, forced priests into hiding, and declared a new state religion to replace Catholicism, named the Cult of the Supreme Being. Normal government, such as the collection of taxes, broke down completely.

Contemporary illustration of the execution of Louis XVI by guillotine

During this period, a group of uncompromising revolutionaries called the **Jacobins** took control of France. Led by Maximilien Robespierre, the Jacobins began a 'reign of terror'. The Jacobins executed anyone suspected of being a **counter-revolutionary** using the **guillotine**.

Guillotines were designed to ensure that all executions were efficient and equal in nature, and were erected in town squares across France. Aristocrats, clergymen, members of the bourgeoisie, and even Robespierre's fellow Jacobins, were taken to meet their fate by the wagonload. In all, 17 000 suspected enemies of the Revolution were sentenced to death during Robespierre's reign of terror, as well as another 23 000 unauthorised killings that are thought to have taken place.

Eventually, opposition to Robespierre's reign of terror grew, and he was arrested and sentenced to death. On 27 July 1794, Robespierre himself was guillotined. The worst of the revolution was now over.

> ### Fact
> In summer 1792, a group of volunteers marched from Marseilles in the south of France to join the French Revolutionary Army. One of their officers wrote a revolutionary anthem for them to sing while marching north. Called the Marseillaise, today it is the French national anthem.

Check your understanding

1. What measures did the National Assembly take during the summer of 1789?
2. Why did the Revolutionaries begin to lose trust in Louis XVI?
3. Why did France declare war on Austria and Prussia in June 1792?
4. In what way was France spiralling out of control by 1794?
5. What was the guillotine?

Unit 3: The French Revolution
The rise of Napoleon

While much of France remained in chaos following the Revolution, the French Revolutionary Army won significant victories across Europe.

Key to these victories was a remarkable young general called Napoleon Bonaparte. Napoleon was born into a family of minor nobility on the French island of **Corsica** in 1769. At the age of nine, he was sent to a military academy in Paris. Here, Napoleon was teased for his Corsican accent, which would have sounded Italian, and made few friends. Instead, he spent his time reading books – particularly on military history.

Napoleon was a 20-year-old junior artillery officer when the French Revolution began. In 1793, Napoleon captured the port of Toulon from a joint force of French royalists and the British army. Napoleon showed such startling military skill in Toulon that as a reward he was made a Brigadier General aged only 24.

In March 1796, Napoleon was placed in command of France's 'Army of Italy'. At the time, northern Italy was ruled by Austria. Showing astonishing military ability, Napoleon defeated the far larger Austrian army, and turned Austria's Italian possessions into republics like France. He returned to Paris a national hero. In 1798, Napoleon launched an even more ambitious campaign to conquer Egypt. Napoleon dreamt of spreading French power east into Persia, like his idol Alexander the Great.

Control of France

Since the death of Robespierre, a 'Directorate' with five members had governed France. The Directorate's rule was muddled and unsuccessful, and by August 1799 it was in crisis. Napoleon's campaign in Egypt was not going well, so when he heard about the political situation in Paris, he abandoned his army and returned to France.

Many people in France were crying out for strong leadership, and Napoleon thought he could provide it. Napoleon staged a coup against the directorate, and was proclaimed First Consul of France in November 1799. At the age of 30, Napoleon was given complete control over French politics.

Napoleon proved to be just as good a political leader as he was a military leader, working tirelessly to bring order back to France. He created the **Napoleonic Code** to rationalise the French legal system. It confirmed many principles of the French Revolution, such as equality before the law and freedom of work. Napoleon also reformed the French education system, rationalised tax collection, and appointed 281 prefects to ensure that his laws were being followed throughout the country.

Painting of Napoleon, aged 23

Painting of Napoleon crossing the Alps in 1800

Painting of Napoleon on his Imperial Throne, completed in 1806

Napoleon also reversed many of the more radical aspects of the French Revolution. In 1801, he made an agreement with the Pope called the **Concordat**, which restored Catholicism as France's major religion. Napoleon also introduced heavy censorship of the press, and published propaganda to promote his own rule.

Nevertheless, many people in France idolised Napoleon for bringing them military victories abroad, and stability at home. In 1804, Napoleon had himself crowned Emperor of the French by the Pope in a lavish ceremony at Notre Dame Cathedral. As Emperor, Napoleon was now more powerful than any monarch in Europe.

Napoleonic wars

The rest of Europe feared the Emperor Napoleon's power and ambition, and Britain, Prussia, Austria, Russia and Sweden all united to defeat him.

However, Napoleon's military tactics, and the fierce loyalty of his enormous French army, proved too much for his enemies. In 1805, Napoleon faced his major rival Austria at the **Battle of Austerlitz**. The combined Austrian and Russian army was 86 000 strong, while Napoleon had only 67 000 troops. Yet once the battle was finished, Napoleon had suffered just 9000 casualties to his opponents' 36 000. At Austerlitz, Napoleon won one of the most decisive victories in the history of European warfare.

Napoleon won more great victories, defeating Prussia in 1806, and Russia in 1807. With each victory, Napoleon signed treaties with the great royal families of Europe, who had to cede land to France or promise loyalty to Napoleon. By 1809, almost all of Europe was either part of the French Empire, allied to France, or governed by a 'puppet' ruler controlled from France. Yet still Napoleon's ambition remained unsatisfied.

Painting of Napoleon at the 1809 Battle of Wagram

Fact

At the age of 26, Napoleon fell deeply in love with Josephine, the daughter of a wealthy Caribbean sugar plantation owner. Josephine was six years older than Napoleon, and her aristocratic first husband was sent to the guillotine during the Terror. Nevertheless, Napoleon married her in 1796.

Painting of Josephine de Beauharnais

Family business

Once Napoleon had conquered a European country, he would often place it under the rule of a family member. Napoleon made his brother Joseph Bonaparte King of Spain, his brother Jerome King of Westphalia, his brother Louis King of Holland, his sister and her husband King and Queen of Naples, and his sister Elisa Duchess of Tuscany. He even made his newborn son King of Rome.

Check your understanding

1. How did Napoleon rise through the ranks of the French Revolutionary Army?
2. How did Napoleon gain control of French politics in 1799?
3. What reforms did Napoleon introduce after he was made first consul?
4. What happened at the Battle of Austerlitz?
5. How much of Europe did Napoleon control by 1809?

Britain's response

At first, many in Britain saw the French Revolution positively. They celebrated France's attempt to move from absolutism to constitutional monarchy, and from feudalism to individual liberty.

The Whig politician Charles James Fox wrote of the revolution, "how much the greatest event it is that ever happened in the world! And how much the best!".

However, as the Revolution became more radical, opinion in Britain polarised. In 1790, a Whig politician called Edmund Burke wrote *Reflections on the Revolution in France*. Burke claimed that the French Revolution was too violent and destructive to succeed. He predicted that the revolution would lead to more bloodshed and military rule, both of which came true.

Mary Wollstonecraft, advocate of women's rights

Burke's book provoked a response from England's best-known radical writer, Thomas Paine. The working class son of a rope maker, Paine helped start the American Revolution with his book *Common Sense*. In 1791, Paine wrote a book celebrating the French Revolution, entitled *The Rights of Man*. Paine criticised monarchy, aristocracy and organised religion, and called for radical political reforms in Britain. One year later, the feminist Mary Wollstonecraft wrote *Vindication of the Rights of Women*, proposing equal education rights for women – an idea that was far ahead of its time.

Following France's declaration of war on Britain in 1793, these ideas quickly lost popularity. British radicals were accused of being dangerous Jacobins, and often attacked. Britain's Prime Minister, William Pitt the Younger, passed laws preventing radical activity. In 1794, Pitt suspended the Habeas Corpus Act, so that suspected political radicals could be imprisoned without trial. In 1795, the Seditions Meetings Act made it illegal to hold a meeting of more than 50 people without a licence.

Statue of Thomas Paine in Thetford, his birthplace

United Irishmen uprising

In 1791, a group of Irishmen inspired by the American and French Revolutions formed the United Irishmen. They hoped to liberate Ireland from British rule with the help of French troops.

In 1796, a French invasion fleet with 15 000 soldiers set sail for Ireland, but was unable to land on its coast due to the bad weather. Tired of waiting for French help, the United Irishmen staged simultaneous uprisings across Ireland in May 1798, led by a Dublin lawyer called Wolfe Tone. The British Army put down the uprising with brutal force, killing 10 000 suspected rebels. Wolfe Tone was captured and sentenced to death. While waiting for his execution in jail, Tone slit his own throat with a razor blade.

The British feared that Ireland could be used as a 'backdoor to Britain' by a French invasion force. To gain more control of the country, Parliament passed the Act of Union in 1800. From January 1801, Ireland became part of a new country called the **United Kingdom of Great Britain and Ireland**.

Fighting Napoleon

In 1803, Napoleon resumed France's plans to invade Britain. He assembled the 'army of Britain' on the French coast, with 165 000 men and 2500 landing craft. Standing on the English coast in Kent with a telescope, it was possible to watch the French invasion force completing their drills. The people of Britain were terrified.

Napoleon knew that to invade Britain, he first needed to gain control of the channel. But to do so, he had to defeat the Royal Navy. The Royal Navy had continued to grow in size, strength and expertise since the 18th century. From the 1790s, sailors were given a daily ration of lemon juice to ward off scurvy. In addition, all British warships now had copper-plated hulls, giving them great speed and endurance at sea.

In October 1805, Britain sent their best Admiral – Horatio Nelson – to defeat the joint French and Spanish navy off the coast of southern Spain. Battle-hardened and famously fearless, Nelson had already lost an eye and an arm in combat.

Nelson engaged the French and Spanish off the Cape of Trafalgar, and sent his ships in two parallel lines towards their fleet. The French and Spanish fleets were devastated, losing 22 ships and sustaining 5781 casualties. The British lost no ships and sustained 1666 casualties. As the battle came to an end, Admiral Nelson died below the deck of his ship the HMS *Victory*, having been shot by a French sniper. Nelson lived just long enough to know that he had won a decisive victory, guaranteeing that Napoleon could no longer launch an invasion of Britain.

> **Fact**
>
> Napoleon became a popular hate figure in Britain. The British ridiculed Napoleon, who was actually of average height, for being short – a myth that persists to this day.

'The Death of Nelson' by Benjamin West, completed in 1806

Check your understanding

1. How did the views of Edmund Burke and Thomas Paine on the French Revolution differ?
2. How did British attitudes towards the French Revolution change after 1793?
3. Why did Parliament pass the Act of Union in 1800?
4. Why did fear of Napoleon in Britain reach its height around 1805?
5. Why was Nelson's victory at the Battle of Trafalgar so important for Britain's safety?

Unit 3: The French Revolution
The fall of Napoleon

In 1810, the Emperor Napoleon was at the height of his power, holding direct or indirect rule over almost all of Western Europe.

When Napoleon defeated Emperor Francis I of Austria in 1809, he asked for the hand of Francis' daughter, Marie-Louise, in marriage. Francis I could not refuse. So having divorced his first wife Josephine, Napoleon married Marie-Louise in April 1810. They had a son the following year.

The only major European power standing outside Napoleon's influence was Britain. In 1806, Napoleon ordered all European nations to stop trading with the British. Napoleon called this economic blockade the **Continental System**, and hoped that it would cripple Britain's economy. Portugal, however, refused to follow the Continental System. In response, Napoleon sent an army through Spain to occupy the Portuguese capital of Lisbon in 1807.

Duke of Wellington, commander of the British forces at the Battle of Waterloo

In 1808, Napoleon forced the King of Spain to **abdicate**, and replaced him with his brother Joseph Bonaparte. But the Spanish people would not accept French rule. Spanish resistance fighters devised a style of combat known as **guerrilla** warfare, meaning 'little wars' in Spanish. Small bands of Spanish rebels, who knew the landscape well, would launch surprise attacks on the French army, and then disappear into the surrounding forests and mountains.

In 1809, Britain sent 30 000 troops to Portugal, under the command of the Duke of Wellington (as he became in 1814). Using Lisbon as a base, Wellington allied with Portuguese and Spanish resistance fighters, and slowly pushed the French out of the Iberian Peninsula.

Napoleon and Russia

In 1810, the Russian Tsar Alexander I abandoned the Continental System and resumed trade with Britain. Napoleon was furious, and began planning an invasion of Russia.

Napoleon amassed an invasion force of 600 000 soldiers, including troops from Prussia, Austria, Poland and Denmark. In June 1812, this enormous force began its advance into Russia. The Russian army did not meet Napoleon, but instead retreated further and further into Russia. As the Russian army retreated, they emptied villages and burned the surrounding fields and food supplies. This **scorched earth** campaign left the French army with little to eat as they advanced.

Saint Basil's Cathedral in Moscow, which survived the fire of 1812

Having marched 590 miles into Russia, Napoleon defeated the Russian army in battle and entered Moscow in September 1812. But he found Moscow deserted, and many of its wooden buildings set on fire. Napoleon and his army were left in an empty, burnt-out shell of a city with no food, and winter closing in. By mid-October, they had no alternative but to begin a gruelling retreat to Western Europe.

The winter was particularly cruel that year, and Napoleon's army spent weeks trudging through the endless snow and frozen expanse of Russia. Troops died of disease, starvation and pneumonia, or were picked off by the Russian cavalry who shadowed their retreat. An estimated 200 000 horses perished – many eaten by the starving troops.

Napoleon abandoned his dying army and returned to Paris on a horse drawn sled. The invincible Emperor had been crushed by the Russian winter. Only one in four of Napoleon's enormous invasion force returned home alive.

Waterloo

Napoleon's catastrophic invasion of Russia was the beginning of the end for the Emperor. One by one, the countries of Europe rose up against French domination.

Painting of Wellington addressing his troops at Waterloo

On 31 March 1814, an allied European army entered Paris, and forced Napoleon to abdicate. He was given the small Mediterranean island of Elba to govern, and sent there to live out the rest of his days. But within a year, Napoleon had escaped exile in Elba, returned to Paris, and raised a new army.

St Helena in the South Atlantic Ocean, where Napoleon was imprisoned

One last time, the nations of Europe united to fight Napoleon. A British and Dutch army under the command of the Duke of Wellington met Napoleon outside the Belgian village of Waterloo on 18 June 1815. The **Battle of Waterloo** was hard fought, lasting for eleven hours. Late in the afternoon, a Prussian army under the command of the 75-year-old General Blücher arrived to reinforce Wellington's troops. The allies were finally able to defeat Napoleon. The Emperor's last stand left Europe with another 47 000 men dead, dying or wounded. When asked about the victory later in life, Wellington said, "It is quite impossible to think of glory…Next to a battle lost, the greatest misery is a battle gained".

Following Waterloo, Napoleon turned himself over to the British. The British imprisoned him in the most remote location they could find: a rocky volcanic island in the middle of the South Atlantic Ocean called **St Helena**. Here, Napoleon lived out the end of his life under the watchful eye of 3000 British troops. In 1821, Napoleon died aged only 51.

> ### Fact
>
> Many of the casualties at Waterloo had their teeth removed to make dentures. So many died that day that well into the 19th century, dentures were still being made using 'Waterloo teeth'.

Check your understanding

1. What was the Continental System?
2. How did the people of Spain respond to French occupation?
3. What tactics did the Russian army employ in order to defeat Napoleon in 1812?
4. What was the result of Napoleon's final battle in Europe at Waterloo?
5. Why was Napoleon exiled to St Helena in 1815?

Unit 3: The French Revolution
Knowledge organiser

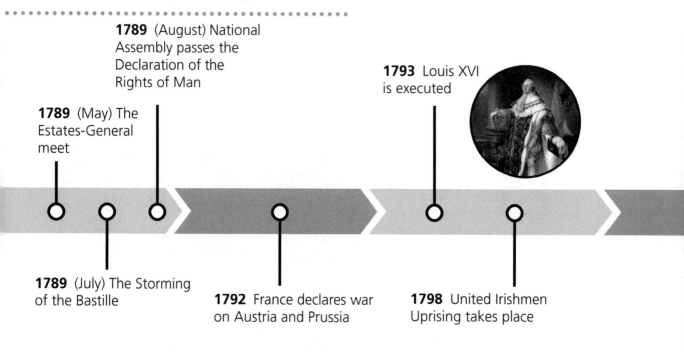

1789 (May) The Estates-General meet

1789 (August) National Assembly passes the Declaration of the Rights of Man

1789 (July) The Storming of the Bastille

1792 France declares war on Austria and Prussia

1793 Louis XVI is executed

1798 United Irishmen Uprising takes place

Key vocabulary

Abdicate To give up one's throne as a monarch

Ancien Régime The established social and political system in France before the Revolution

Bastille Medieval fortress in the centre of Paris, stormed by mob at the start of the Revolution

Battle of Austerlitz Decisive victory for Napoleon against Russia and Austria in 1805

Battle of Trafalgar Decisive victory for the Royal Navy against France in 1805

Battle of Waterloo The final defeat of Napoleon in 1815

Bourgeoisie French middle-class, or those who make money through trade or industry

Concordat Agreement between Napoleon and the Pope, signed in 1801

Continental System Europe-wide economic blockade against Britain led by Napoleon

Corsica Mediterranean island off the south coast of France, birthplace of Napoleon

Counter-revolutionary Someone fighting against a Revolution, to restore the previous system

Declaration of the Rights of Man Document guaranteeing the rights and freedoms of all French citizens

Estates-General Meeting of France's clergy, aristocracy and bourgeoisie to consult on policy

Guerrilla A small, independent fighting force used to raid and attack a larger army

Guillotine Machine designed to behead people, associated with the French Revolution

Jacobin A radical group of French Revolutionaries who used violence to defend the revolution

Napoleonic Code French legal system established in 1804

National Assembly Breakaway group formed by France's Third Estate in June 1789

Polarise Process whereby public opinion divides, and is driven towards two extremes

Prussia Large princely state in what is now northeast Germany

Radical Person who advocates widespread social or political reform

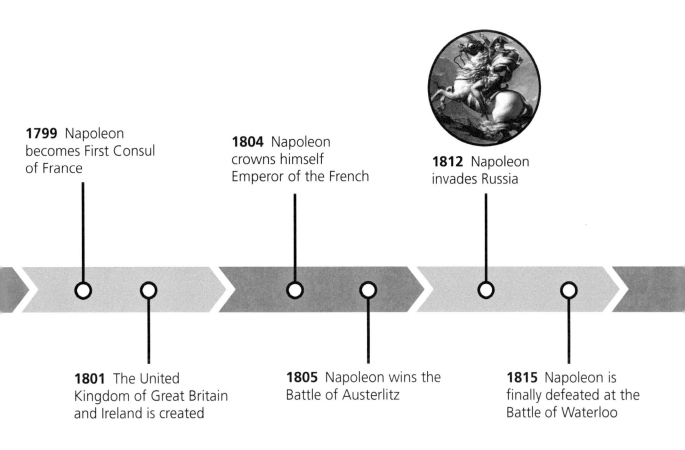

1799 Napoleon becomes First Consul of France

1804 Napoleon crowns himself Emperor of the French

1812 Napoleon invades Russia

1801 The United Kingdom of Great Britain and Ireland is created

1805 Napoleon wins the Battle of Austerlitz

1815 Napoleon is finally defeated at the Battle of Waterloo

Key vocabulary

Revolutionary Person participating in a revolution

Sans-culottes Radical French revolutionary, often from a lower-class background in Paris

Scorched earth Military strategy of destroying own land to disadvantage an invading force

St Helena Volcanic island in the South Atlantic, and place of final exile for Napoleon

The Terror Period of mass political executions during the French revolution, from 1793–94

United Kingdom of Great Britain and Ireland New country created by the 1800 Act of Union

Versailles Magnificent royal palace, home to the French monarchy

Key people

Duke of Wellington Commander of the allied army at Waterloo, later Prime Minister

Horatio Nelson British Admiral at the Battle of Trafalgar

Louis XVI King of France at the time of the French Revolution

Marie Antoinette Austrian wife of Louis XVI

Mary Wollstonecraft Feminist and author of *Vindication of the Rights of Women*

Maximilien Robespierre Revolutionary leader during 'The Terror'

Napoleon Bonaparte French military and political leader, from 1799 to 1815

Thomas Paine 18th century British radical, author of *The Rights of Man*

Wolfe Tone Leader of the United Irishmen uprising

Unit 4: The Industrial Revolution
The steam engine

For the whole of its history up until the 18th century, humankind had depended upon the natural world for power.

Ships used the wind in their sails to cross seas, and mills harnessed the wind to grind grain into flour. Some early factories used water power to carry out tasks such as **spinning** raw cotton into thread. But these factories could only be built beside fast moving rivers, often in remote valleys. The great majority of **industry** and manufacturing, and all land transport, were carried out using human or animal strength.

Newcomen

Thomas Newcomen was an ironmonger from Devon. Along with Cornwall, Devon was home to Britain's richest copper and tin mines. As Newcomen would have known, 18th century mines were prone to flooding, frequently drowning the miners who worked in them.

To solve this problem, Newcomen created a **steam engine** capable of pumping water out of a mine. Newcomen's steam engine contained a single cylinder that filled with steam, which was then rapidly cooled by a burst of cold water injected into the cylinder. As the cylinder cooled, the steam turned into water, causing it to reduce to 1/1600 of its original volume. This rapid change of state created a vacuum, which pulled a **piston** at the top of the cylinder downwards. This motion was then harnessed to pump water out of the mine.

In 1712, Newcomen built his first steam engine in a West Midlands coalmine. By 1769, there were around 100 Newcomen engines being used across the north of England and Scotland.

However, Newcomen's steam engine was not efficient, as the furnace that produced the steam required huge quantities of coal. The great majority of Newcomen steam engines were used to pump water out of coalmines, where the necessary fuel was abundant and effectively free. When Newcomen died in 1729, his obituary described him as, "sole inventor of that surprising machine for raising water by fire". Few could have predicted the world-changing potential that his invention held.

Boulton and Watt

James Watt was a Scottish engineer, who specialised in making medical instruments. In 1764, he was asked to fix a Newcomen engine owned by the University of Glasgow. Watt was transfixed by the engine, and began designing a more efficient version, requiring less coal.

Watt observed that the cylinder in Newcomen's engine repeatedly needed to be heated, then cooled, then reheated.

The windmill was a pre-industrial source of power

Drawing of a Newcomen steam engine at work in Lancashire

Portrait of James Watt

This process wasted huge amounts of energy. So, Watt started to design a steam engine with a separate **cold condenser** attached to the cylinder for cooling the steam, which allowed the cylinder to remain permanently hot.

For eleven years, Watt struggled to make his cold condenser work. In 1774, he moved from Glasgow to **Birmingham**, to become business partners with a wealthy factory owner called Matthew Boulton. While Watt could be rather gloomy, Boulton was a cheery, optimistic man. With the help of Boulton's money and encouragement, Watt built his first two functioning steam engines in 1776. One was used to pump water out of a coalmine in Staffordshire, the other to power bellows for a **blast furnace** in Shropshire.

Painting of one of Watt and Boulton's steam engines pumping water out of a coal mine, 1790s

Newcomen's first engine in 1712 required 20 kilograms of coal per horsepower hour, while Watt's first engine required just 2 kilograms of coal per horsepower hour. Watt's steam engine was significantly more efficient, and demand spread throughout Britain. When James Boswell visited Matthew Boulton's factory in Birmingham in 1776, Boulton told him: "I sell here, sir, what all the world desires to have – power".

In 1781, Watt and Boulton devised a method for turning the 'up and down' motion of their engine into a rotation motion using a 'sun and planet gear', which spun a large wheel. This innovation greatly expanded the steam engine's potential. Engineers could now develop more uses for steam engines, such as lifting heavy materials, pressing oils from seeds, and crushing sugar. By 1800, there were 451 in use across Britain. Over the course of the 19th century, the power created by steam engines was harnessed to weave textiles, harvest wheat, power trains, print newspapers, and eventually create electricity.

James Watt died aged 83, a very wealthy man. His steam engine had liberated humankind from its dependence on wind, water and muscle as sources of power, by unlocking the energy within fossil fuels. More than any other invention, Watt's steam engine can be said to have created the industrial revolution.

> ### Fact
>
> Watt struggled for years to build his first steam engine, and suffered frequent bouts of self-doubt. In January 1771, Watt wrote in his diary, "Today I entered the 35th year of my life & I think I have hardly done 35 pence worth of good in the world but I cannot help it."

Check your understanding

1. What was Newcomen's first steam engine used for?
2. Why was it cost effective to use Newcomen's steam engine in coal mines?
3. How did James Watt's steam engine improve on the design of Thomas Newcomen?
4. What purposes were Watt's first two steam engines used for?
5. What purposes were Watt's steam engines used for during the 19th century?

Unit 4: The Industrial Revolution
Cotton textiles

Before the industrial revolution, all manufactured goods were made by hand. Today, most goods we purchase are produced by machines.

The first product to be mass-produced by machines was cotton. Creating cotton textiles involves two processes. First, the raw cotton fibres are twisted and wound to create thread, a process known as spinning. The thinner and stronger the thread, the more valuable it became. Since the 13th century, cotton had been spun in England using a spinning wheel, which twists and winds thread onto a wooden rod called a spindle.

The next process is **weaving**. Textiles are produced by stretching threads lengthways, known as the warp, and interleaving them with a widthways thread, known as the weft. **Handlooms** had been used to weave textiles in Britain since the Roman period.

During the 18th century, women and children in poor farming communities earned extra money by spinning cotton. Cotton thread would then be taken to a single adult, usually a man, operating a handloom in his own house. For this reason, the production of textiles was known as a **cottage industry**.

Photograph of a pre-industrial spinning wheel

Mechanisation

James Hargreaves was an illiterate handloom weaver from Lancashire, who wanted to find a more efficient process for spinning cotton. In 1764, Hargreaves invented a spinning wheel that could feed eight spindles at once, greatly increasing the amount of cotton thread one person could produce. Hargreaves nicknamed his machine 'jenny' (short for engine), so it became known as the **spinning jenny**.

The next breakthrough came from a Bolton wig maker called Richard Arkwright. In 1769, Arkwright invented a water-powered machine that could spin multiple strands of cotton thread, and named it the 'spinning frame'.

The spinning jenny spun thread that was fine in texture, but weak and snapped under pressure. Arkwright's **water frame** spun thread that was strong, but coarse. In 1779, a cotton spinner from Bolton called Samuel Crompton built a machine combining the best aspects of both inventions. Because combining a donkey and a horse produces a mule, Crompton named his invention the **Crompton mule**.

In 1785, one of Boulton and Watt's newly invented steam engines was used to power a Crompton mule for the first time, and the amount of cotton thread produced in Britain exploded. One factory worker overseeing a spinning mule could produce **exponentially** more cotton than one cotton spinner sitting at a spinning wheel, and the cost of fine cotton thread dropped by 90 per cent in the ten years from 1785 to 1795.

Richard Arkwright, inventor of the spinning frame and pioneer of the factory system

Around this time, the **powerloom** was invented by attaching Boulton and Watt's steam engine to a loom. It took longer for the powerloom to be perfected, but their number increased from 2400 in 1813, to 115 600 in 1835, to 250 000 in 1857. At the same time, the number of individual handloom operators dropped from a peak of 240 000 in 1820, to just 3000 by 1862.

Print showing steam-powered cotton spinning in a cotton mill, 1825

The factory

Richard Arkwright was not just a brilliant inventor, he was also a shrewd businessman. In 1775, Arkwright opened a five-storey water mill beside the Derwent River in Cromford, Derbyshire, to house his water frames. The **Cromford Mill** went on to employ 800 people, and many claim it was the world's first modern factory. Arkwright built more factories across Staffordshire, **Manchester** and Scotland, creating an industrial empire. He died in 1792 one of the wealthiest men in Britain, having amassed a personal fortune of £500 000.

Arkwright's **factory system** took employment out of cottages, and into large purpose-built structures, designed to house heavy machinery operated by hundreds, sometimes thousands, of workers. This would transform the way that humans worked throughout the western world during the 19th century.

By 1800, there were 900 cotton mills in Britain. Most were in Lancashire, which provided an ideal location for the production of cotton textiles. Lancashire's abundant coalfields powered the steam engines, Liverpool's port supplied raw cotton from the Americas, and the damp climate prevented cotton thread from snapping under pressure. At the centre of this trade was Manchester. Nicknamed 'Cottonopolis', Manchester grew from a small market town of 10 000 people in 1720, to a world city of 380 000 people in 1860.

Due to the **mechanisation** of cotton production, Britain could sell cheaper, better cotton textiles than anywhere else in the world. British cotton exports grew from £248 000 during the 1770s, to £29 million during the 1820s – comprising an astonishing 62 per cent of all British exports. India had dominated the world trade in cotton textiles during the previous century, but by the 1820s its renowned handmade textiles could no longer compete with Britain's factory-made alternative.

Fact

These new inventions scared families who earned money using spinning wheels and handlooms. In 1767, cotton spinners broke into James Hargreaves' house and destroyed his spinning jennies, forcing him to move to Nottingham. Nine years later, Richard Arkwright's new watermill outside Chorley was burnt down.

Check your understanding

1. What does the term 'cotton industry' mean?

2. How did Hargreaves and Arkwright's inventions improve the efficiency of cotton spinning?

3. How did the application of steam power to cotton manufacturing change the cost of textiles?

4. Why was Lancashire an ideal location for the production of cotton textiles?

5. How did mechanisation allow Britain to dominate the world trade in cotton textiles?

4.2

Unit 4: The Industrial Revolution
Iron and coal

Factories and steam engines burnt through vast quantities of coal. Fortunately for Britain, some of the world's richest coal reserves lay beneath its soil.

Britain was already mining 80 per cent of the total volume of coal used in Europe by 1700, well before the industrial revolution began. That year, 2.7 million tons of coal were mined, and used for tasks as varied as heating houses, baking bricks and tiles, evaporating water in salt pans, and brewing beer.

Mining coal, however, was notoriously dangerous. Men, women and children dug coal with pickaxes in mines up to 100 m below ground, travelling down narrow shafts to reach them. In these primitive mines, miners were in constant danger of being suffocated by lack of air, drowned by sudden influxes of water, buried by collapsing mineshafts, or blown up when their candle flames came into contact with pockets of methane.

Illustration of work underground in the Bradley mine in Staffordshire, 1850s

Transporting coal was expensive. People in London used coal mined in Durham and Newcastle, in northeast England. This coal was transported via the North Sea, but was five times more expensive once it arrived in London. For this reason, all of Britain's major industries developed beside natural coal reserves. In 1800, a total of 15 million tons of coal were mined in Britain, and the highest regional producers were:

- The northeast with 4.5 million tons
- The west midlands with 2.5 million tons
- Central Scotland with 2 million tons
- South Wales with 1.7 million tons
- Lancashire with 1.4 million tons.

These regions became the heartlands of British industry. For the next 150 years, coal was used to fire their furnaces, power their steam engines, heat their forges, pump their water, and drive their trains. In 1850, a total of 50 million tons of coal were mined in Britain, rising to 250 million by 1900.

Iron

Since the 16th century, cast iron had been produced in Britain using blast furnaces. Blast furnaces heated iron ore with charcoal, a fuel created by carbonising wood. Air was blasted through the furnace base using water-powered bellows, causing the mixture to reach 1300 °C. At this temperature, molten iron could be released through a tap at the base of the furnace.

'Iron and Coal' by William Bell Scott, 1861

Blast furnaces supplied Britain's pre-industrial metalworks with iron to make items such as cooking pots, nails, buttons, pins, cannons, guns and locks. But by 1700, Britain was running out of suitable trees with which to make charcoal, and had to import iron from Sweden and Russia.

Painting of the blast furnace at the ironworks in Coalbrookdale running through the night, 1801

Abraham Darby was born in 1678 on a farm in Dudley, where his father ran a small iron forge. Darby realised that if he could use coal, not charcoal, to fuel a blast furnace, he could produce abundant supplies of cheap iron. But the impurities in coal, such as water, tar, sulphur and gas, created iron that was weak and useless.

In 1708, Darby leased a blast furnace in Coalbrookdale, Shropshire. Here, Darby baked his coal in sealed ovens to drive off the impurities, creating a high-carbon fuel called **coke**. In 1710, Darby successfully used coke to produce strong, workable cast iron for the first time. This transformed iron production in Britain.

By 1720, coke-powered blast furnaces produced 400 tons of cast iron, increasing to 76 000 tons by 1788. When Britain's industrial revolution began at the end of the 18th century, a ready supply of iron was needed to construct steam engines, factory machines and railway tracks. Darby's invention from 1710 made this possible.

The invention of cast iron demonstrates the way in which the major inventions of the industrial revolution helped each other to keep on improving. For example, the famous ironmaster John Wilkinson (see box) built the precision cast iron cylinders for James Watt's steam engine. In return, Watt's second ever working steam engine was installed at Wilkinson's Shropshire ironworks in 1776 to power the bellows. This allowed Wilkinson to produce cheaper, better quality iron, which in turn allowed Watt to build more steam engines.

John 'iron mad' Wilkinson

Wilkinson was a successful ironmaster, who made a fortune supplying cast iron cannons to the Royal Navy during the Seven Years' War. Wilkinson had an extreme dedication to building products from iron, earning him the nickname 'iron mad'. He built an iron pulpit for his local Methodist church, paid his employees with iron tokens, and was buried in an iron coffin. Wilkinson's grave is still marked by an enormous iron obelisk today.

Fact

By 1779, Abraham Darby's ironworks were owned by his grandson Abraham Darby III. That year, Darby III built a 100 metre bridge over the River Severn. It was the world's first iron bridge, situated just one mile from his grandfather's original ironworks in Coalbrookdale.

Check your understanding

1. Why was coal being mined in Britain before the industrial revolution began?
2. Why did Britain have to import much of its iron from abroad by 1700?
3. Why were so many factories built near coalmines during the industrial revolution?
4. What was Abraham Darby's invention, and how did it increase cast iron production in Britain?
5. What iron objects did John 'iron mad' Wilkinson build during his career?

Unit 4: The Industrial Revolution
Transport

Transporting heavy goods long distances overland was not easy during the pre-industrial age.

Where possible, goods such as timber, coal, iron, slate and bricks were transported along navigable rivers, which reduced the cost of transport. But where no such rivers were available, goods had to be pulled along roads by a horse-drawn cart. And where no roads were available, goods had to be carried on the back of a **packhorse**.

Canals

The genius of a **canal** is simple. At the very most, a packhorse can carry 150 kg of coal. However, if coal is loaded onto a barge, and that barge is floated in a canal, then the same horse can pull up to 300 000 kg of coal. Canals therefore dramatically increased the volume of goods that could be transported across Britain.

Britain's first major canal project began in 1759. The Duke of Bridgewater owned a large coalmine on his land in Worsley, Lancashire. He wanted to find a more efficient means of transporting the coal ten miles away to its main market in Manchester. So he enlisted an expert engineer called James Brindley to build a canal.

Photograph of a horse-drawn barge pulling heavy goods along a canal

At first, canals could only travel along flat land, so Brindley had to build a large aqueduct over the Irwell River valley, and dig tunnels beneath parts of central Manchester. Many ridiculed Brindley's project, but when the Bridgewater Canal opened in 1761 it immediately halved the cost of coal in Manchester. Before long, every mine, ironworks and factory in Britain wanted a canal built beside it.

By 1850, Britain had a network of 4000 miles of canals. Canal design became increasingly advanced, carrying barges up and down hills using complicated systems of locks and gates. Though many canals eventually lost business to the railway, they continued to be widely used by industry right up until the 1940s.

The steam train

The most advanced form of pre-industrial passenger travel was the stagecoach, but even this was slow, uncomfortable and expensive. Some improvements were made by running horse-drawn carriages along railway tracks, speeding up and smoothing out the journey. This was particularly useful for transporting heavy loads in coalmines and ironworks.

Richard Trevithick was an engineer from Cornwall. In 1804, Trevithick built a steam engine attached to a railway cart, which was able to drive itself forwards. Trevithick had built a functioning steam train, but it could only

Portrait of George Stephenson

travel at 2.4 miles per hour. Engineers such as Trevithick who worked on steam train technology met frequent problems. Early steam trains used up too much coal, frequently broke down, and caused railway tracks to buckle under their weight.

It took a brilliant engineer called George Stephenson to perfect the design. Stephenson was born into a poor Newcastle mining family in 1781. Nevertheless, Stephenson started learning to read and write at the age of eighteen, and became a self-taught engineer.

In 1829, a group of Liverpool and Manchester industrialists ran a competition for engineers to design a train capable of travelling the 35 miles between their two cities. Three steam trains were entered, including George Stephenson's train, the **Rocket**. Stephenson's train was the clear winner, reaching a top speed of 30 miles per hour.

Replica of Stephenson's *Rocket*, in Leicestershire

On 15 September, 1830, the Liverpool to Manchester Railway held its grand opening. Around 800 people boarded the first train from Manchester to Liverpool with enormous excitement, including the Prime Minister, the Duke of Wellington. Another passenger was the novelist Frances Ann Kemble. She later wrote, "I never enjoyed anything so much as that first hour of our progress". The Liverpool to Manchester Railway was the world's first fully functioning inter-city railway service. Britain's 'Railway Age' was now underway.

Navvies

The labourers who built Britain's canals and railways were known as navigators, or **navvies**. They dug thousands of miles of canals and railway lines with tools no more advanced than a shovel and a pickaxe. It was backbreaking and dangerous labour, often attracting young men from Ireland who came to Britain looking for work.

Navvies lived in temporary camps alongside their constructions, and gained a reputation for hard working, hard living and hard drinking. Nevertheless, the work was well paid for manual labour, and by the 1840s there were 200 000 navvies building railways across Britain.

Fact

The Liverpool MP William Huskisson was invited on the maiden journey of the Liverpool to Manchester Railway. He did not know, however, that another train was travelling in the opposite direction. When Huskisson's train stopped for water, he stepped out of his carriage and into the path of an oncoming train. Huskisson died later that day in hospital.

Check your understanding

1. Why were canals so efficient at transporting heavy goods across Britain?

2. What was the impact of the Duke of Bridgewater's canal opening in 1761?

3. What challenges did the early steam trains face?

4. Which steam train won the 1829 competition to travel between Manchester and Liverpool?

5. What was working life like for those people who built the railways?

Unit 4: The Industrial Revolution
The Railway Age

Before Stephenson's *Rocket*, the fastest that any human had travelled on land was at the speed of a galloping horse.

By the 1840s, however, trains were regularly reaching speeds of 60 miles per hour. During this decade, Britain went through a period called **Railway Mania**, as private companies competed to build railway lines across the country. By 1850, 6100 miles of railway track had been laid, rising to 14 510 miles by 1875. Soon, every major town and city in Britain was connected by rail.

Painting of the crowds at Paddington Station in London, 1862

Life sped up

People living in Victorian Britain felt their country shrink due to the railways. Journeys that once took days to complete now only took hours. In 1780, it took 19 hours to travel from London to Bristol by stagecoach. In 1841, it took just four hours by train.

By 1891, trains carried almost 900 million passengers a year, and the average person in Britain took a train every other week. Trains reflected the Victorian class system. First-class carriages had carpets and cushioned seats, while second-class carriages had basic seating. Third-class carriages were simply open-air carts, until Parliament regulated in 1844 that all carriages had to be covered.

Painting of two women in a train carriage, 1862

Before the train, the time in Britain could vary by up to 20 minutes from location to location. This caused problems when train companies wanted to write accurate timetables. In 1847, a standard time was set throughout Britain according to Greenwich Mean Time. Railways also changed Britain in unexpected ways. Once seafood could be caught and transported inland within a day, fish and chips became one of Britain's favourite dishes. Professional football became possible, as teams could travel the country competing in a national league.

Not everybody welcomed the railway. Farmers objected to having railway lines built through their land, and some claimed that trains frightened their cows, turning the cows' milk sour. Britain's once thriving stagecoach business disappeared almost overnight, leaving roads empty and coaching inns abandoned. In 1860, the novelist William Thackeray wrote that the "pre-railroad world… has passed into limbo and vanished".

Fact

In 1841, a Baptist Minister called Thomas Cook organised a train excursion from Leicester to Loughborough. Cook organised more excursions, and went on to found a successful company that remains one of Britain's best-known travel companys.

Five Days' Trip to the West of England
T. Cook, Excursion Agent, Leicester, has great pleasure in announcing to the friends of temperance

CHARMING EXCURSION
CHELTENHAM, GLOUCESTER,
BRISTOL,
EXETER & PLYMOUTH.
TUESDAY, JUNE 18, 1850,
SPECIAL TRAINS

During the 1840s, communication between train stations was achieved by sending electrical signals down metal **telegraph** cables, which ran alongside railway lines. The public began paying to send messages, known as telegrams, along these cables. This allowed near-instant electronic communication to be sent around Britain. In 1866, Brunel's **SS *Great Eastern*** (see box) laid a telegraph cable along the seabed of the Atlantic Ocean. News could now travel from New York to London in a matter of minutes.

Trains contributed to Britain's rapid economic growth during the 1850s and 1860s, by cutting the cost of transporting goods. Cities could become increasingly specialised in their particular trades. Sheffield was known for its steel, Bradford for its woollen textiles, and Stoke-on-Trent for its ceramics. Birmingham had many small factories producing different products, earning its name 'the city of one thousand trades'. One of Birmingham's best-loved trades was chocolate, produced by the Cadbury family.

The majority of these goods produced in Britain were sold abroad. Mid-Victorian Britain was known as the 'workshop of the world'. This global economic dominance was gained in part through the British Empire, but also through being the first nation in the world to industrialise. By the 1870s, however, industrialisation in rival countries was catching up. As the 19th century came to an end, Germany and the United States had become the world's leading industrial nations, and Britain was slipping behind.

Brunel

Isambard Kingdom Brunel was the most prolific engineer of the Railway Age. Over his career, he designed and built railway lines, train stations, bridges, tunnels, dockyards and steamships.

Brunel's work ethic was intense: he slept only four hours a night, and smoked 40 cigars a day. Aged 27, Brunel began work on the Great Western Railway line. To keep the line direct, Brunel used charges of dynamite to blow a tunnel beneath Box Hill in the Cotswolds, killing many navvies in the process. When it was finished, the Box Hill tunnel was the longest in the world.

Later in his career, Brunel turned his mind to building trans-Atlantic steamships, but his ambition was also his downfall. In 1853, Brunel began work on the SS *Great Eastern,* a gargantuan steamship that remained the longest in the world for the next 40 years. It left its builders bankrupt, and suffered an explosion on its maiden voyage. Exhausted from his work, Brunel died two weeks after the *Great Eastern's* launch in 1859.

Check your understanding

1. Why was Britain said to have 'shrunk' due to the railways?

2. Why did the railways lead to standardised time in Britain?

3. What form of electronic communication spread around Britain due to the railways?

4. What impact did the railways have on everyday life in Britain?

5. What were Isambard Kingdom Brunel's achievements as an engineer?

Unit 4: The Industrial Revolution
Knowledge organiser

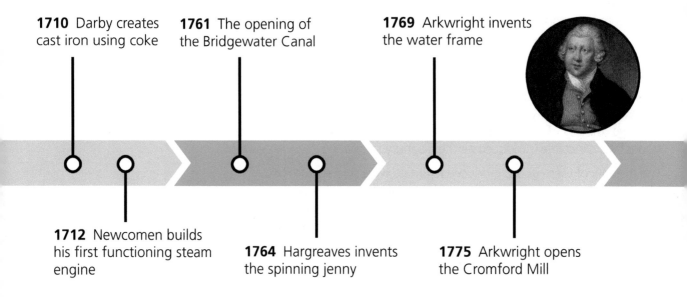

1710 Darby creates cast iron using coke

1761 The opening of the Bridgewater Canal

1769 Arkwright invents the water frame

1712 Newcomen builds his first functioning steam engine

1764 Hargreaves invents the spinning jenny

1775 Arkwright opens the Cromford Mill

Key vocabulary

Birmingham West Midlands industrial hub, known as the 'city of one thousand trades'

Blast furnace Brick or stone tower in which iron ore is heated with coke to create cast iron

Canal Manmade waterway, often built to transport heavy goods

Coke A fossil fuel with high carbon content and few impurities, created by heating coal

Cold condenser Key component of the Watt steam engine which greatly improved its efficiency

Cottage industry Small-scale business or manufacturing taking place in people's homes

Cromford Mill Cotton mill built by Richard Arkwright, said to be the first factory in Britain

Crompton mule Invention that combined the spinning jenny and the water frame to spin cotton

Efficiency Achieving maximum productivity with minimum wasted energy or expense

Exponential A growth that becomes increasingly rapid as it grows

Factory system Form of work that involves large workforces, large buildings and machinery

Handloom Hand operated machinery, used to weave textiles in Britain since the Roman period

Industry The processing of raw materials into manufactured or consumable goods

Manchester Centre of Britain's cotton industry, nicknamed 'Cottonopolis'

Mechanisation Introduce machines to a process to make it more efficient

Navvies 19th century labourers involved in the construction of a road, railway or canal

Packhorse A horse used to carry heavy loads on its back

Piston A disk fitted into a cylinder, moving up and down – crucial component of a steam engine

Powerloom Mechanised loom for weaving cotton driven by a steam engine

Railway Mania Period of enthusiastic railway building during the 1840s in Britain

Rocket Steam train built by George Stephenson to travel between Liverpool and Manchester

Spinning Process of twisting and winding raw cotton fibres to create thread

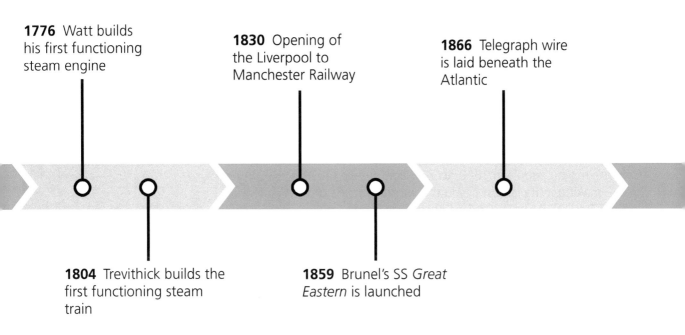

1776 Watt builds his first functioning steam engine

1830 Opening of the Liverpool to Manchester Railway

1866 Telegraph wire is laid beneath the Atlantic

1804 Trevithick builds the first functioning steam train

1859 Brunel's SS *Great Eastern* is launched

Key vocabulary

Spinning jenny Machine created by James Hargreaves to spin eight cotton threads at once

SS *Great Eastern* Largest steamship in the world, designed by Brunel and completed in 1859

Steam engine Machine that uses the expansion or condensation of water to generate power

Telegraph System for transmitting messages along a wire using an electrical signal

Water frame Machine created by Richard Arkwright using water power to spin cotton

Weaving Process of interleaving threads, such as cotton, wool, linen or silk, to make textiles

Key people

Abraham Darby Ironmaster who pioneered the use of coke, made from coal, to create cast iron

George Stephenson Engineer who built the first public railway, famous for his train the *Rocket*

Isambard Kingdom Brunel Celebrated Victorian engineer, built the Great Western Railway

James Hargreaves Handloom weaver from Lancashire who designed the spinning jenny

James Watt Engineer who designed an efficient steam engine with wide commercial use in 1776

John Wilkinson Famous ironmaster who designed the cylinders for Watt's steam engine

Richard Arkwright Industrialist who designed the water frame, and built many factories

Richard Trevithick Cornish engineer who designed the first working steam train

Unit 5: The Age of Reform
Urbanisation

Britain's 1851 census revealed that – for the first time in the country's history – over half the population lived in a town or a city.

The factory system drove **urbanisation** in 19th-century Britain. In contrast with cottage industries, factories require hundreds, even thousands, of **labourers** to live side by side.

Painting of the view towards Manchester from Kersal Moor, 1852

The growth of Britain's cities was staggering. London grew from one million people in 1810, to 7 million people by 1911 – making it the largest city in the world. Outside of London, Britain's largest cities had once been medieval trading centres such as York and Norwich, but they were overtaken by industrial centres such as Liverpool and Glasgow (see table). Some towns grew out of nothing. Middlesbrough was a small farming village of 25 people in 1801. It then began producing iron and steel, and by 1861 it was a large town of 19 000 inhabitants.

City	1801 population	1851 population
Liverpool	82 000	376 000
Glasgow	77 000	357 000
Manchester	75 000	303 000
Birmingham	71 000	233 000
Leeds	53 000	172 000

Overcrowding and disease

As labourers flocked from rural villages to industrial towns, the supply of houses could not keep up with demand. Many families ended up living in conditions of severe overcrowding. Sometimes multiple families shared a single room. An 1847 investigation revealed that on Church Lane in London's East End, 1095 people lived in 27 houses – an average of 40 to a house. The poorest new arrivals to industrial cities lived in rented cellars. These miserable living spaces were dark and cold, lacked fresh air, had floors made of mud, and often flooded.

Photograph of slum housing in Kensington, London. Late 19th century

Poorly built terraced houses were built to meet the never-ending demand. **Back-to-back** houses were tightly packed into a small area, and had no back yard and little natural light.

At the start of the 19th century, only the wealthiest people's homes had running water and sewers. For the poor, a whole street of houses had to share a single water pump and toilet. In some cities, inhabitants had to get their water from their river, which would also be used as a sewer and dumping ground for waste such as animal carcasses. Diseases such as typhus, tuberculosis, and cholera spread with ease. The death rate for industrial towns increased from 19 out of every 1000 people in 1831, to 25 out of every 1000 people in 1849.

Public health

Whose role was it to clean up Britain's cities? Some Victorian social reformers believed that towns should have their own local government, able to raise taxes and use that money for public services. This contradicted the popular Victorian assumption that such activity was best carried out by private individuals or businesses, a philosophy known as *laissez faire* government.

Social reformers used statistics to challenge these *laissez faire* assumptions. The best-known reformer was Edwin Chadwick, who wrote *The Sanitary Conditions of the Labouring Population* in 1842. Chadwick showed a clear link between poor living conditions, and disease and death. His survey discovered that the life expectancy of a labourer in rural Rutland was 38, compared with just 17 in the industrial city of Manchester.

Such findings shocked the British government into action. Like many Victorians, Chadwick believed that disease was spread by bad smells, known as 'miasma' (the germ theory of disease only emerged during the 1860s). Though incorrect, miasma theory did suggest that dirt, decay and waste should be cleared from Britain's towns and cities.

The 1835 Municipal Corporations Act introduced elected town councils, which were the first form of local government in many industrial towns. In 1875, Parliament passed the Public Health Act, making it compulsory for town councils to establish sewers, drainage, and a clean water supply.

In London, the civil engineer Joseph Bazalgette built 82 miles of sewers between 1859–1875. These sewers linked to a large sewer beneath the Thames embankment, which pumped human waste all the way to the sea.

By the end of the 19th century, life in Britain's cities had improved significantly. In 1901, 77 per cent of Britain's population lived in towns and cities. With their trams, trains, suburbs, street lighting, high streets, professional football clubs and public parks they were not so different to the cities we still inhabit today.

Fact

A long hot summer in London in 1858 caused the human and industrial waste on the banks of the Thames to heat up. The smell was so horrific that it was known as the **Great Stink**. Parliament had to be suspended due to the smell, and eventually Joseph Bazalgette was commissioned to construct new sewers (see below).

Photograph of public health reformer Edwin Chadwick

Check your understanding

1. Why did the industrial revolution cause Britain's cities to grow so rapidly?
2. Why were living conditions so bad in many of Britain's industrial towns?
3. Why did diseases spread with such ease in Britain's industrial towns?
4. How did Edwin Chadwick challenge the government's *laissez faire* assumptions?
5. How did the public health of British cities improve during the 19th century?

Unit 5: The Age of Reform
Factory life

Britain's farmers and rural labourers were attracted by the promise of greater pay in Britain's rapidly growing factories, mills, dockyards, and mines.

The work of a rural labourer moved with the weather and the seasons, with different jobs worked at different times of the year. In contrast, industrial workers performed specialised, repetitive tasks throughout the year. Punctuality was strictly enforced, often by a factory bell.

Britain's early factories could be dangerous and brutally unpleasant places to work. Many labourers worked 12- to 14-hour days, six days a week. When demand for products boomed, this could increase to 19 hours. The noise of the machines caused workers to lose their hearing, and the dust and cotton fibres that filled the air caused lung diseases.

The distant relationship between farmer and landowner was replaced by the closer, and often bitter, relationship between worker and factory owner. Factory owners kept strict discipline, docking the wages of employees who broke factory rules.

Fact

At the Belper Mill in Derbyshire, a list was kept between 1803 and 1815 of all the workers who had their wages docked for breaking factory rules. Offences included: 'leaving his dust room dirty'; 'Throwing bobbins at people'; 'Terrifying S Pearson with her ugly face' and 'Throwing water on Ann Gregory very frequently.'

Child labour

During the early 19th century, poor families depended upon the extra income provided by their children. In industrial areas, the average age for a child to be sent to work was just eight and a half. Some children started work as young as five.

In cotton mills, children worked as **scavengers**, crawling beneath the spinning mules to collect loose cotton. Or they worked as **piecers**, fixing snapped threads. Children had to work right next to moving machinery, and if their arms or leg got caught, they could lose a limb. Factory foremen would beat children with a leather strap for not working hard enough, or for being disobedient. The strain of this physical labour on children's developing bodies caused stunted growth and lifelong deformities, such as knock-knees or a bent spine.

Illustration of a child labourer being beaten in a London string factory, 1848

The worst treatment was reserved for children without families, who factory owners purchased from parish orphanages and **workhouses**. One such child was Robert Blincoe, who aged seven was taken from a London workhouse to work as a scavenger in a Nottingham cotton mill. As an adult, Blincoe wrote his memoirs of life as a factory child. He recounted working 14-hour days, fed on porridge and black bread. Disobedient children, Blincoe recalled, were placed in iron shackles.

By the early 1840s, around 20 000 children worked in Britain's coalmines. The youngest children worked as **trappers**, opening and closing ventilation doors. Older children mined narrow seams, dragging heavy carts on their hands and knees through tunnels less than 50 centimetres high. Coalmines could be horrifically dangerous (see pages 46–47). In 1838, heavy rains flooded the Huskar Pit near Barnsley, drowning 26 children.

Illustration of a woman and two children hauling coal through a mineshaft in 1848

One of the worst jobs for a Victorian child was chimney sweep's apprentice, or **climbing boy**. Climbing boys were often orphans, given to work for chimney sweeps by parish authorities. They had to climb inside the narrow chimneys of coal fires and brush away the soot. At first, a climbing boy's knees and elbows would cut and stream with blood, so chimney sweeps rubbed the boy's wounds with salt-water to toughen up the skin. Working as a climbing boy could be fatal, as they risked becoming trapped in the chimneys, or choking to death on the soot.

Luddites

Before the industrial revolution took place, Britain's textile weavers were highly skilled and well paid artisans. However, their handcrafted textiles could not compete with the low prices of textiles made by machines.

In November 1811, Nottingham stocking makers broke into factories at night. Armed with sledgehammers, they destroyed the newly invented stocking frames that were putting them out of work. Stories spread of the Nottingham weavers, and their mythical leader 'Ned' or 'General' Ludd. His followers became highly organised, and known as **Luddites**.

In 1812, Luddite attacks took place in Lancashire, where handloom weavers broke into factories and destroyed the newly installed powerlooms. In Yorkshire, wool workers destroyed shearing frames, and Luddites even turned to assassination. In April 1812, a Yorkshire wool manufacturer was shot dead while riding across a moor to his mill in Marsden.

Parliament took firm action. The destruction of factory machinery was made punishable by death in 1812, and 10 000 troops were sent north to put down disturbances. Around 70 Luddite leaders were executed, and many more were transported to Australia. Though Luddites were mainly concerned with protecting their livelihoods, today the term 'Luddite' is used to describe people who oppose new technologies.

Check your understanding
1. How did the work of an industrial worker differ from that of a rural labourer?
2. Why were cotton mills such dangerous places for children to work?
3. What work did child labourers have to perform in coalmines?
4. Why was work as a climbing boy so dangerous?
5. What inspired Luddites to attack factories and machines from 1811–12?

Unit 5: The Age of Reform
Social reform

During the early 19th century, it was commonly assumed that employers should be free to treat their employees how they chose.

Some industrialists tried to improve their employees' wellbeing. However, most factory owners were more concerned with profits than employee welfare. Industrialists saw their factories as private property and in line with the *laissez faire* assumptions of the day, they believed the government had no right to interfere.

Lord Ashley

By 1830, support was growing in Parliament for factory reform. A Tory aristocrat called Anthony Ashley Cooper, the 7th Earl of Shaftesbury, became its champion. Lord Ashley was an evangelical Christian, with a profound humanitarian drive. Parliamentary committees and a Royal Commission were established to investigate child labour in factories, and they uncovered horrific stories of cruelty and abuse.

Anthony Ashley Cooper, the 7th Earl of Shaftesbury

In 1833, Parliament passed the Factory Act, making it illegal for textile factories to employ children under the age of nine. Children under 13 could only work eight hours a day, with two hours set aside for schooling. Most importantly, four full-time factory inspectors were employed to make sure the law was enforced.

In 1840, Lord Ashley introduced an act of Parliament banning the use of climbing boys. In 1842, he helped Parliament pass the Mines Act, prohibiting coalmines from employing women or girls, and boys under the age of 10. Many more Factory Acts were passed throughout the Victorian period, placing further limits on workers' hours and greatly improving factory safety.

Workers' rights

At first, workers could do very little to improve their own pay and conditions. The Combination Act of 1799 made it illegal for workers to combine and form trade **unions**. This prevented them from making collective demands, or from striking to make sure their demands were met. The Combination Acts were repealed in 1824, leading to a growth in union organisations.

The first great campaign for workers' rights originated not in the industrial north, but in rural Dorset. Here, the accepted minimum wage for a farmer was 10 shillings a week. But in the village of Tolpuddle, a group of farm labourers had their wage of 9s a week cut to 7s, with threats that it would fall further to 6s. In response, six farm labourers formed a **Friendly Society** – similar to a union – in 1833. Each of them took part in a secretive initiation ceremony, which involved being blindfolded and swearing an oath of loyalty.

> ### Fact
>
> To increase support for the Mines Act, Lord Ashley published an illustrated report of the Royal Commission into child labour in coalmines. It revealed that young girls would work alongside men in a state of semi-nudity, due to the heat of the mines. The British public were horrified.

In response, a local landowner and magistrate had the six men arrested and charged with taking 'unlawful oaths'. The men were found guilty, and transported to Australia in 1834 for seven years' hard labour.

The harshness of this sentence outraged working people across Britain, and the six men became known as the **Tolpuddle Martyrs**. In April 1834, an estimated 25 000 workers marched on London asking for the Martyrs' sentence to be overturned, and delivered a petition with 800 000 signatures to the Prime Minister. Two years later, the Home Secretary granted a free pardon to the Tolpuddle Martyrs. Between 1837–39, the six labourers returned to their families in Dorset, and to celebrations across the country.

Illustration of the workers' march on London, April 1834

The workhouse

Since the Tudor period, local parishes had dealt with the poor and unemployed by paying them financial 'relief'. By the early 1830s, the cost of parish relief had risen to £7 million per year. Social reformers suspected that relief was encouraging able-bodied workers to become lazy, and avoid finding employment.

In 1834, Parliament passed the Poor Law Amendment Act, which ended the payment of relief to able-bodied workers. Instead, they were given work and employment in newly-built workhouses. However, to discourage the poor from claiming relief in workhouses, conditions were deliberately made unpleasant.

Photograph of women having lunch in St Pancras workhouse in London, 1901

Families were split up, with different areas for men, women and children. Inmates had to sleep in large dormitories, and wear prison-style uniforms. Work consisted of hard, menial jobs such as breaking stones, and inmates were not allowed to smoke, drink alcohol, or keep personal possessions. The Victorian poor lived in constant fear that misfortune might land them in the workhouse.

In 1846, a scandal emerged from the Andover workhouse. The workhouse master was a former army sergeant and violent drunk, who sold the workhouse food and left its inmates starving. Inmates were made to crush bones to make fertiliser, and were found trying to feed themselves by sucking rotting marrow from inside the bones.

Despite such scandals, workhouses continued to operate, and were only formally abolished in 1930.

Check your understanding
1. How did Lord Ashley's reforms improve working conditions for industrial workers?
2. Why were the Tolpuddle Martyrs transported to Australia in 1834?
3. How did British workers ensure the Tolpuddle Martyrs were pardoned?
4. How did the 1834 Poor Law Amendment Act change the way the poor claimed relief?
5. Why were workhouse conditions made so unpleasant?

Unit 5: The Age of Reform
Political reform

In 1832, Britain had a population of 16 million people, but only 400 000 people (2.5 per cent of the population) had the right to vote for a Member of Parliament.

Most of these voters were wealthy property owners, and all of them were male. But because Britain's **electoral system** had been evolving since the medieval period, the right to vote varied enormously across the country.

In **rotten boroughs**, just one family or landowner had the power to choose the MP. The most notorious rotten borough was Old Sarum, which was once a thriving market town, but had been an uninhabited hillside since the 17th century. Nevertheless, a group of local landowners still got to choose two Old Sarum MPs for Parliament.

Cartoon showing Whig reformers cutting down a rotten tree, representing the old political system

In contrast, many of Britain's growing industrial cities had never been given representation in Parliament. Birmingham, Manchester, Sheffield and Leeds were four of the largest cities in Britain, but none of them had their own MP.

In boroughs where a large number of people had the right to vote, candidates would spend a fortune buying voters' support with bribes, food and alcohol. In addition, there was no **secret ballot**. This meant voting took place in public, so landowners could intimidate their tenants to vote a certain way. This messy and corrupt political system meant Parliament did not serve the interests of the common people. Power remained firmly in the hands of the aristocracy.

Great Reform Act

Inspired by the American and French Revolutions, political radicals in Britain campaigned for an end to corruption and aristocratic government. Radicals gained support from the middle class, and also from Britain's growing **working class**.

In 1831, a Whig politician called Earl Grey became Prime Minister. Although he was an aristocrat, Grey was a long-time supporter of political reform. His government proposed to extend the vote to every man living in a property worth £10 or more, and to abolish 60 of Britain's smallest boroughs, redistributing their MPs to industrial regions.

Grey's Reform Bill was accepted by the House of Commons, but rejected by the House of Lords. Earl Grey resigned, and the people of Britain were furious. Riots erupted across the country. An angry mob burnt a castle belonging to the Duke of Newcastle to the ground, and in Birmingham a radical named Thomas Attwood promised to raise 100 000 armed men to march on London. The House of Lords changed their minds, and Earl Grey's **Great Reform Act** passed in 1832.

Fact

In 1819, around 60 000 people gathered in St Peter's Field in Manchester to listen to the well-known political radical called Henry Hunt. Ten minutes into his speech, the local yeoman cavalry charged into the crowd with their swords drawn. Their attack left 11 people dead, and another 500 injured. The event became known as the 'Peterloo Massacre'.

Portrait of Whig Prime Minister Earl Grey

Chartists

The Great Reform Act was a landmark in British history, but many believed it did not go far enough. It only increased Britain's **electorate** to 650 000 people, all taken from the wealthy middle class. So, in 1838, a group of working class radicals led by William Lovett, a London cabinetmaker, wrote the People's Charter. It contained six demands for further political reform:

1. Universal male **suffrage**
2. Equal electoral districts
3. Removal of property qualifications for MPs
4. Payment of MPs
5. Secret ballot
6. Annual elections

Supporters of Lovett's demands became known as the 'Chartists'. Britain entered a harsh economic depression during the 1840s, and support for **Chartism** grew. The Chartists presented repeated petitions to Parliament signed by millions of working people, but Parliament refused to debate their demands. In 1848, the Chartists held their largest meeting on Kennington Common in south London, attended by as many as 50 000 supporters.

The Chartists movement died away after 1848, but Lovett and his radicals had a significant impact on British politics. By 1918, all but one of the demands on the People's Charter had been achieved.

Chartists meet on Kennington Common, London, 1848

Further reform

Campaigns for political reform returned during the 1860s. In Parliament, members of the Liberal party were its strongest supporters. However, in 1867 a Conservative Prime Minister called Benjamin Disraeli cleverly decided to adopt the policy. Disraeli's Second Reform Act gave one million more men the right to vote, earning a huge boost in support for the Conservative party.

VOTES FOR WOMEN.

Mrs. PANKHURST

The leader of the Liberal Party, William Gladstone, was furious that Disraeli had stolen his policy. Gladstone was a giant of Victorian politics, who served in parliament for over 60 years and was Prime Minister on four separate occasions. In 1884, Gladstone finally achieved his own reform, passing the Third Reform Act. This extended the vote to all male homeowners, around two in five of Britain's male population.

Photograph of Emmeline Pankhurst, who campaigned for women to have the right to vote

It would take another 50 years, however, before women in Britain were given the right to vote on the same basis as men.

Check your understanding

1. What was messy and corrupt about Britain's electoral system before 1832?
2. What happened at St Peter's Field in Manchester in 1819?
3. What happened when the House of Lords rejected Earl Grey's Reform Bill?
4. Why did William Lovett and his fellow radicals write the People's Charter?
5. Who was William Gladstone, and what did his Third Reform Act achieve?

Law and order

Throughout history, urbanisation has been associated with increases in crime and social disorder. Britain in the 19th century was no different.

In Britain's rural towns and villages, small communities were largely able to police themselves. But this was not the case in the growing cities of the industrial revolution. As towns and cities filled with inhabitants who were strangers to one another, crime became more common.

Industrial change also caused periodic waves of unemployment, leading to riots and lawlessness. In 1812, Spencer Perceval became Britain's first and only Prime Minister to be assassinated, shot dead by a dispossessed businessman.

Crime was a growing public concern in early 19th-century Britain. Statistics published by the government appeared to show increases in crime throughout the 1830s and 1840s. In 1843, it was reported in the House of Commons that the loss of money from robbery and theft in Liverpool had totalled £700 000 in one year.

Criminal activity centred on **rookeries**, areas of slum housing made up of dark, narrow alleyways and dilapidated buildings. Some of the worst rookeries were in London, with names such as Jacob's Island, Rat's Castle, and the Devil's Acre. In 1839, Charles Dickens described a London rookery containing 'men and women, in every variety of scanty and dirty apparel, lounging, scolding, drinking, smoking, squabbling, fighting, and swearing.'

The police

Robert Peel was the son of a Lancashire cotton manufacturer, and a brilliant politician. At the age of 34 he was appointed Home Secretary.

In 1829, Peel passed the **Metropolitan Police** Act, establishing a force of 1000 full-time London policemen. London already had around 450 unpaid parish **constables**, but they were too disorganised and few in number to cope with the city's crime. In contrast, the Metropolitan Police were centrally managed from a head office in Whitehall called Scotland Yard.

Metropolitan Police constables had to be over 5 foot 7 inches, and were given a uniform of blue tailcoat, belt, and a metal-lined top hat. Their tailcoats had stiff collars, designed to prevent the officers from being strangled. Peel insisted that the Metropolitan Police should not be seen as a military force, so they were armed with truncheons instead of guns. Policemen were soon nicknamed 'bobbies', or 'peelers', in honour of their founder.

> ### Fact
> There were many slang terms for criminals in Victorian London, such as magsman (confidence trickster), cracksman (burglar), hositer (shop-lifter), fogle-hunter (pick-pocket), sharper (card trickster), and swell mob (a gang of well-dressed thieves).

Portrait of Sir Robert Peel

In 1856, police forces were made mandatory across all of England. This caused resentment and riots in some towns by those who saw the police as a sign of government tyranny. Nevertheless, by 1900, Britain had 47 000 policemen working across 243 separate forces.

Though crime statistics are difficult to trust, it is generally believed that crime decreased during the second half of the 19th century. From 1861 to 1891, the proportion of arrests per 1000 of London's population fell from 20 to 15. Britain's annual murder rate fell from 1.7 per 100 000 people during the 1860s, to 1 per 100 000 people during the 1890s.

Prison reform

In 1813, a Quaker **philanthropist** called Elizabeth Fry visited Newgate, one of London's most notorious prisons.

Fry was outraged by what she saw: 300 female prisoners cooking, washing, and living in just two cells. They were poorly clothed, and slept on the floor lined with straw. Some were even looking after newborn babies, naked and crying with the cold. The following day, Fry returned with food and clothing for the women.

Fry encouraged Newgate Prison to establish a school for prison children, and keep female prisoners occupied with productive work such as sewing and knitting. She travelled the country campaigning for prison reform, and became an expert on the subject. In 1818, a Parliamentary commission was established to investigate prison conditions, and Fry was invited to present evidence to Parliament – the first woman in British history to do so.

Robert Peel greatly admired Elizabeth Fry. Her campaigns inspired him to pass the 1823 Gaols Act, which introduced prison inspections, visits from doctors, schools for prison children, and payment for jailers. Until then, jailers had their wages paid by the prisoners themselves! Fry died in 1845, known and admired throughout Europe as a visionary social reformer.

Victorian illustration of Elizabeth Fry reading the Bible to women imprisoned in Newgate Jail

Jack the Ripper

Between August and November 1888, five prostitutes were murdered and brutally disemboweled in the Whitechapel area of East London. After the first two murders, Scotland Yard received a letter claiming to be from the killer, boasting about the murders and mocking the police. The letter ended, "Good Luck. Yours truly, Jack the Ripper".

The case of Jack the Ripper transfixed the Victorian public, but the murderer was never arrested. Jack the Ripper's identity is still debated to this day.

Check your understanding

1. Why was crime a growing public concern in early 19th century Britain?
2. What did Robert Peel's 1829 Metropolitan Police Act create?
3. What happened to crime rates during the later 19th century?
4. How did Elizabeth Fry help to improve the treatment of prisoners in Britain's jails?
5. What crimes did Jack the Ripper commit?

Unit 5: The Age of Reform
Knowledge organiser

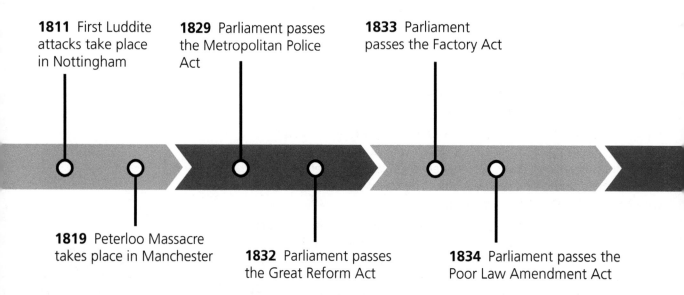

1811 First Luddite attacks take place in Nottingham

1829 Parliament passes the Metropolitan Police Act

1833 Parliament passes the Factory Act

1819 Peterloo Massacre takes place in Manchester

1832 Parliament passes the Great Reform Act

1834 Parliament passes the Poor Law Amendment Act

Key vocabulary

Back-to-back Cheaply built terraced house with no back yard and little natural light

Chartism Working class movement for equal political rights that began in 1838

Climbing boy Child labourer made to climb chimneys and sweep away the soot

Constable First rank in the British police force

Electoral system Set of rules by which representatives are elected to Parliament

Electorate All of the people in a country or state entitled to vote in an election

Friendly Society An association of workers designed for helping one another

Great Reform Act Landmark political Act that began the reform of the British Parliament

Great Stink Long hot summer in 1858, which caused the Thames to smell so badly that Parliament had to be suspended

Labourer Someone who performs unskilled manual work for a wage

laissez faire Government policy of leaving society to function with little intervention

Luddite Textile weavers and artisans who attacked factories and destroyed machines

Metropolitan Police Britain's first professional police force, established in London in 1829

Philanthropist A person who works or gives money to improve the lives of others

Piecer Child labourer made to fix snapped threads in a cotton mill

Rookery Victorian city slum, often inhabited by criminals

Rotten borough Electoral borough where one family or landowner chooses the MP

Scavenger Child labourer made to crawl below spinning machines and collect loose cotton

Secret ballot An election in which votes are not cast in public

Suffrage The right to vote in political elections

Tolpuddle Martyrs Six Dorset farm labourers who became the focus of a campaign

Trapper Child labourer made to open and close ventilation doors in a coalmine

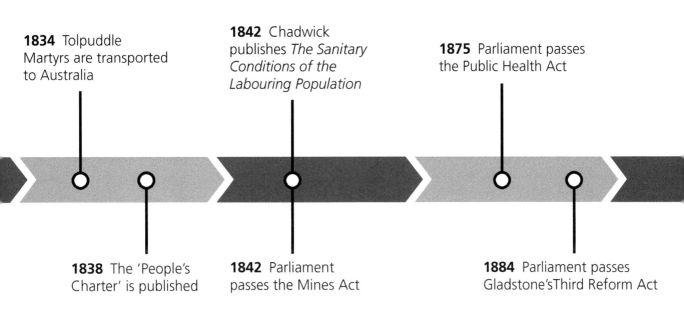

1834 Tolpuddle Martyrs are transported to Australia

1842 Chadwick publishes *The Sanitary Conditions of the Labouring Population*

1875 Parliament passes the Public Health Act

1838 The 'People's Charter' is published

1842 Parliament passes the Mines Act

1884 Parliament passes Gladstone'sThird Reform Act

Key people

Anthony Ashley Cooper 7th Earl of Shaftesbury and Victorian champion of social reform

Earl Grey Whig Prime Minister who passed the 1832 Great Reform Act

Edwin Chadwick Social reformer who used statistics to link poverty with disease

Elizabeth Fry Quaker philanthropist who led a campaign to reform Britain's prisons

General Ludd Mythical leader of attacks on factories and machines by textile workers

Jack the Ripper Murderer who operated in Whitechapel, still unidentified to this day

Robert Peel Tory Home Secretary and Prime Minister, who founded the Metropolitan Police

William Gladstone Liberal Prime Minister who passed the Third Reform Act

William Lovett London cabinetmaker and leader of the Chartists

Key vocabulary

Quaker Christian religious movement which emphasises charity and social justice

Union An association of workers formed to pursue collective rights and interests

Urbanisation Growth in the population of urban areas, often caused by inward rural migration

Workhouse Institution built to provide work and accommodation for the poor and unemployed

Working class Group in society who carry out urban, industrial jobs for a wage

Queen Victoria

Queen Victoria inherited the throne from her uncle William IV in 1837. She was just eighteen years old, and stood at 4 foot 11 inches.

Portrait of Queen Victoria, 1859

Many members of the Royal Court hoped to rule on the young Queen's behalf, in particular her overbearing mother the duchess of Kent. But Victoria was an independent minded queen, and immediately took charge of her royal affairs.

In 1840, Queen Victoria married her first cousin, a German prince named Albert. Victoria and Albert loved each other deeply, and they had nine children together over the next seventeen years. Albert took a particular interest in industry and political reform (see box, right), and Victoria placed a lot of trust in his political judgement.

Queen Victoria set about restoring public faith in the Royal Family, which had become very unpopular during the reign of her Hanoverian uncles. Victoria toured Britain on the newly invented steam train, became a patron of numerous institutions and charities, and presented the Royal Family as an ordinary and loving family unit.

Portrait of Queen Victoria and her family, 1846

However, tragedy struck in 1861 when Prince Albert died aged just 42. Queen Victoria was paralysed by sadness, and disappeared from public life for the next ten years. The British public began to turn against their absent Queen, who they nicknamed the 'widow of Windsor'.

Queen Victoria slowly returned to public life during the 1870s. She was reinvigorated by her responsibilities as Queen, and took a particular interest in the British Empire. In 1876, Victoria's favourite Prime Minister –Benjamin Disraeli – convinced her to adopt the title 'Empress of India'. Though Victoria never visited India, the region fascinated her. One of Victoria's favourite companions was an Indian servant named Abdul Karim, who instructed her on Indian affairs and taught her phrases in Urdu and Hindi.

By the end of the 19th century, Victoria had come to symbolise the British Empire: a living embodiment of Britannia. Across the world, hospitals, universities, cities, waterfalls and entire provinces still bear her name. Queen Victoria's influence on public life was so great that the character and outlook of 19th-century Britain – from its emphasis on moral uprightness to its confidence in Empire and belief in progress – became known as 'Victorian'.

Public opinion

The British public began to take a much closer interest in the British Empire during Queen Victoria's reign. Much of this was due to technological improvements.

Fact

When Queen Victoria died, she was Britain's oldest and longest reigning monarch. This was quite an achievement, considering that she survived at least six assassination attempts during her lifetime.

Travel to the colonies became far quicker from the 1840s onwards due to the steamship. By 1880, almost 100 000 miles of telegraph cable had been laid beneath the ocean, giving people in Britain near-instant communication with its colonies. British newspapers could offer up to date reports on the British Army's campaigns in faraway locations such as Afghanistan, Burma and the Sudan. They did so with great excitement.

Celebrated British Army officers, such as 'Gordon of Khartoum', became household names. An army nurse called Florence Nightingale devised innovations to improve conditions for British soldiers injured whilst fighting in the Crimea. As a result, she became one of the most celebrated figures in Victorian Britain. Another hero of Empire was the Christian **missionary** David Livingstone, who explored much of southern Africa during the 1850s and 60s.

Contemporary illustration of Queen Victoria's Diamond Jubilee Parade in 1897

During the late 19th century, many British people began to believe that they had the right to rule other nations due to their racial superiority. Native populations, be they Maoris, Bengalis or Zulus, were frequently likened to children, or labelled 'savages'. A distorted version of Charles Darwin's Theory of Evolution was used to argue that British Anglo-Saxons were superior in intelligence and morality to the races they governed.

In 1897, Queen Victoria celebrated her Diamond Jubilee. A great procession travelled through London, with representatives from across the Empire. It included Canadian Hussars, Cypriot policemen in fezzes, and the Maharajas of Hindu princely states. Four years later, Queen Victoria died aged 81.

The Great Exhibition

In 1851, Prince Albert helped to organise an international exhibition, celebrating industry and manufacturing. The **Great Exhibition** was housed in a temporary building in Hyde Park, constructed from a cast-iron frame and 294 000 panes of glass. Named the **Crystal Palace**, the completed building was 108 feet tall.

The Great Exhibition contained 100 000 different exhibits from around the world, including a folding piano, the world's largest diamond, and early prototypes of the bicycle and typewriter. Six million people visited the exhibition from Britain and abroad, many taking day trips to London along newly built railway lines. On 1 May 1851, Queen Victoria opened the exhibition. She recorded in her diary, 'This day is one of the greatest and most glorious of our lives'.

Check your understanding

1. How did Queen Victoria restore Britain's faith in the Royal Family?

2. How did Queen Victoria come to symbolise the British Empire?

3. What was the Great Exhibition?

4. How did technological change alter the British public's awareness of Empire?

5. How did theories of racial supremacy change British attitudes towards Empire?

Indian Rebellion

During the 19th century, the power of the East India Company continued to grow at an astonishing rate.

British rule expanded into the Marathas, Burma, Punjab, Sind, Berar, and Oudh. By 1857, the East India Company ruled almost the entire Indian subcontinent. Some princely states remained independent, but their Hindu princes still had to rule in accordance with British policy.

British rule in India

During the eighteenth century, the East India Company had little interest in changing Indian society. On the contrary, Company officers were well known for marrying Indian women, adopting local customs, and learning languages such as Hindi, Persian and Urdu.

This changed during the 19th century. The twin spirits of evangelical Christianity and Liberal reform in Britain crossed over into India. Many in the East India Company now believed they should not just tax and trade with India, but should also improve and Christianise India. In 1813, a ban on Christian missionaries working in India was lifted. British evangelicals could now travel to India and convert its Hindus and Muslims to Christianity.

Railway station in Mumbai, India. Completed in 1888, it was initially named Queen Victoria Terminus, but has since been renamed Chhatrapati Shivaji Terminus

In 1828, Lord Bentinck became the new Governor General of the East India Company. Bentinck wanted to stop Indian customs that he perceived as uncivilised. He worked to eradicate *thagi*, a cult of assassin-priests (known as 'thugs' – the origin of today's word) who ritually murdered and robbed travellers. In 1829, Bentinck also banned the practice of **sutti**. This was a Hindu custom whereby widows were encouraged to commit suicide by throwing themselves on their husband's funeral pyre.

The British also saw it as their role to modernise India. They built post offices in all major Indian towns, along with hospitals and schools – which prepared young Indian children for the **civil service** with a largely British curriculum. By 1858, the British had laid nearly 300 miles of railway track in India, and 4000 miles of telegraph lines for speedy communication.

Indian Rebellion

By 1857, the British Indian Army contained 40 000 British troops, and 230 000 Indian troops, known as **sepoys**. There was a growing discontent among the *sepoys* about British rule in India, which boiled over in May 1857.

In the town of Meerut, the British had imprisoned 85 *sepoys* who were refusing to follow British orders. In response, four *sepoy* regiments decided to **mutiny** against British command. They destroyed the British army base,

Illustration of sepoys in the British Indian Army, around 1860

murdered the British officers and their families, and freed the imprisoned *sepoys*. From Meerut, the *sepoys* marched to Delhi, gaining support for the rebellion along the way. A force of 40000 Indians took control of Delhi, and proclaimed the aged prince Bahadur Shah, a descendent of the Mughals, Emperor of India.

The Indian Rebellion was strongest in the north of India, where rebels took control of the towns of Cawnpore, Agra and Lucknow. Rumours spread – some true, some false – of Indian atrocities. In Cawnpore, 120 British men, women and children were killed by Indian troops, and had their mutilated bodies hidden in a well. But with no clear leadership or aim, the Indian Mutiny soon lost momentum.

The British response was uncompromising. In September 1857, the British Indian Army retook Delhi, and those suspected of supporting the mutiny were executed on the spot without a trial. In Peshwar, 40 mutineers were strapped to cannons and blown apart. In Cawnpore, the corpses of executed Indian rebels were hung from trees, to serve as a warning to others. Some historians estimate that 100000 Indians were killed in the aftermath of the rebellion.

Contemporary illustration of Indian sepoys being blown apart by British cannons

The British Raj

The faith of Victorian Britain in its Empire was severely shaken by the events of 1857, and the Indian Rebellion led to significant reforms to British rule in India.

The East India Company was dissolved in 1858, and India became directly ruled through a viceroy, who was appointed by Queen Victoria. The British promised Indians working in the British Indian Army and the Indian civil service that they would gain the same promotion opportunities as their British counterparts. And the emphasis of British rule moved back to celebrating, instead of attempting to reform, Indian traditions and customs.

The period of British rule in India after 1857 became known as the **Raj** –from the Hindi for 'reign'. For the next 90 years, British rule in India gained a renewed confidence. India came to be regarded as – in the words attributed to the Prime Minister Benjamin Disraeli – the 'jewel in the crown' of the British Empire.

Fact

The imprisoned *sepoys* in Meerut had refused to fire their new Enfield rifles on parade due to a rumour that the cartridges were sealed with pig and cow fat. Soldiers had to bite their cartridges open to load their rifles. Muslim and Hindu *sepoys* saw this as an insult to their religious views.

Check your understanding

1. How did British rule in India change from the 18th to the 19th century?
2. What Indian customs did Lord Bentinck try to reform once made Governor General?
3. How did the Indian Mutiny begin?
4. How did the British respond to the Indian Mutiny?
5. How did British rule in India change after the Indian Mutiny?

Unit 6: The Victorian Empire
Ireland and Home Rule

First invaded by the Norman kings during the 12th century, Ireland is sometimes said to have been Britain's first colony.

By the 18th century, a two-tier society had developed in Ireland. A ruling class of Protestant landowners descended from British settlers held much of the wealth and power. But they governed a population that was 80 per cent Catholic.

Though ruled by Britain, Ireland remained a separate country with its own Parliament in Dublin. In 1798, a group of political radicals known as the United Irishmen rose up and demanded Irish independence from British rule (see pages 36–37).

Abandoned sod roof cottage in West Ireland

The British did not want to see Ireland become independent, so they passed the Act of Union in 1800. This Act ruled that Ireland was no longer its own country, but instead part of a new country called the United Kingdom of Great Britain and Ireland. From January 1801, Ireland was governed directly from London, and lost its Parliament in Dublin.

After 1801, many of Ireland's Protestant landowners no longer had to attend Dublin's Parliament, so they moved to Britain. They became known as Ireland's **absentee landlords**, and were accused of neglecting their Irish farmland, and mistreating their Irish **tenants**.

During the 1800s, very little money was invested in Irish industry – with the exception of shipyards in Belfast. While Britain became the wealthiest country in the world, much of Ireland remained desperately poor. Sixty per cent of the population lived in sod houses, made of little more than earth.

The Irish potato famine

Potatoes can be grown in a high volume on a confined patch of land, which suited the small plots that Irish farmers rented from their landlords. Since its arrival in Europe from South America, the potato had become the staple diet for much of Ireland's population. By 1845, the Irish were consuming some 7 million tonnes of potatoes per year.

Then, in the summer of 1845, some of Ireland's potatoes began to rot in the ground, turning into black, inedible slime. A potato blight had hit Ireland, which destroyed one third of that year's harvest. In 1846, the blight spread even further. Three quarters of the potato harvest was destroyed that year, and again in 1847.

Contemporary illustration of a starving boy and girl looking for food in West Cork

News spread to England that the Irish people were dying in their thousands, and whole towns were being lost to starvation, malnutrition and disease. In the summer of 1846, the British government bought large quantities of American maize to feed Ireland's population, and reduced the tax on foreign grain imports. In January 1847, Parliament voted through the Soup Kitchen Act, which provided soup kitchens to feed 3 million of Ireland's population.

But these measures were too little and too late. The Potato Famine was the worst social disaster to strike any European nation during the 19th century. By 1852, one million people had died in Ireland. Over the next 25 years, another three million Irish men and women emigrated, mostly to the United States.

Irish Home Rule

Many in Ireland blamed the Potato Famine on British rule, causing bitter resentment of the British for generations to come. This contributed to a growth of support for Irish independence. In 1858 Irish nationalists formed a secret organisation called the **Irish Republican Brotherhood**, and in 1867 they exploded a bomb in London, killing 12 people. In Ireland, there was growing social unrest. Some tenant farmers murdered their landlords or burnt down their stately homes, while others boycotted the payment of rent.

Contemporary illustration of Irish emigrants waiting to board a boat to America

Many in Britain and Ireland saw a policy known as **Home Rule** as the solution to Irish unrest. Though not full independence, Home Rule proposed the reversal of the 1800 Act of Union, allowing Ireland once again to have its own Parliament in Dublin.

By the end of the 19th century, Home Rule was the most controversial issue in British politics. In 1885, the Liberal Prime Minister William Gladstone became a supporter of Home Rule. This led to members of his Liberal party splitting to join the Conservatives.

Opponents of Irish Home Rule feared the policy would be the first step towards the break-up of the whole British Empire. Gladstone introduced his second Home Rule Bill to Parliament in 1893. It passed in the Commons, but was defeated in the Lords – where many of the members owned land in Ireland. Home Rule had failed, but the question of who should govern Ireland did not go away. Conflicts only became fiercer as the 20th century began.

Fact

Due to famine and emigration, Ireland's population dropped from 8.5 million in 1845 to 4.5 million in 1901. Today, Ireland has still not regained its pre-famine population levels, and deserted 'famine villages' can be seen across the country.

Check your understanding

1. How did the 1800 Act of Union change Irish politics?

2. What were the consequences of the 1800 Act of Union for Irish society?

3. Why was the potato blight so destructive in Ireland?

4. What did Britain do to relieve the potato famine in Ireland?

5. What was Home Rule, and why did it fail?

Unit 6: The Victorian Empire
The Scramble for Africa

Until the end of the 19th century, Europe's colonial powers paid little attention to Africa.

Then, in a burst of activity between 1880 and 1900, European powers took control of 90 per cent of Africa's territory. By the end of the century, Britain, France, Germany, Italy, Belgium, Portugal and Spain all had African colonies. This period came to be known as the 'Scramble for Africa'.

Modern photograph of the Suez Canal

Egypt and the Sudan

In 1869, the **Suez Canal** opened in Egypt. This waterway linked the Mediterranean Sea with the Indian Ocean (via the Red Sea), and was co-owned by Egypt and France. It made Egypt, and its capital Alexandria, a vital centre of world trade.

In 1875, Egypt was in financial trouble, so Britain bought its 44 per cent share in the Suez Canal for £4 million. Then in 1882, a popular uprising took place in Egypt, which threatened Britain and France's Egyptian investments. So the British Army invaded Alexandria. The Egyptian ruler Tewfik Pasha was restored, but he now led a **puppet government** under the control of a British Consul-General.

Through Tewfik Pasha, Britain gained informal rule over Egypt. This drew them into a conflict in the Sudan. Here, followers of a radical branch of Islam called the Mahdists had revolted against Egyptian rule. So, in 1898, a British–Egyptian army led by General (later Lord) Kitchener set out to retake the Sudanese town of Khartoum.

Lord Kitchener, who won fame as an army officer at the Battle of Omdurman

Kitchener assembled his army on the banks of the River Nile, beside a plain called **Omdurman**. He had under his command 8000 British and 12 000 Egyptian soldiers, who faced an enormous force of 52 000 Mahdist soldiers. Armed with spears, swords and outdated rifles, the Mahdists were no match for advanced British weaponry. At the ensuing Battle of Omdurman, 10 000 Mahdist soldiers were killed, and 13 000 injured, compared with just 429 casualties on the British–Egyptian side.

Elsewhere in Africa, British rule spread through government sponsored private enterprises. In the west of the continent, the United African Company was founded to take advantage of the lucrative palm oil trade. This led to the formation of the British colony of Nigeria in 1900. On Africa's east coast, an ambitious Scotsman called William McKinnon established the Imperial British East Africa Company. By 1895, this company had helped spread British control to Uganda, Kenya, Zanzibar, Pemba and British Somaliland.

> ## Fact
>
> An important factor for securing Britain's military victories in Africa, such as the Battle of Omdurman, was the **Maxim gun**. Invented in 1883, it was the world's first machine gun. A member of the Matabele tribe, who fought the British in 1893, described Maxims as 'guns that spat bullets as the heavens sometimes spit hail'.

Cape Colony

Positioned at the tip of South Africa, **Cape Colony** was an important stopping point for European ships trading with Asia. Britain gained Cape Colony from the Dutch in 1814. With it came a population of 27 000 descendants of Dutch settlers, known as **Boers**.

The Boers were fiercely independent farmers and strong Protestants, who spoke a Dutch dialect they called Afrikaans. After disagreements with their new British governors, the Boers trekked inland and established two independent Boer states within Cape Colony during the 1830s. They were named **Transvaal** and the Orange Free State.

Mining for diamonds in Colesberg, Cape Colony, 1872

At first, the British showed little interest in large-scale settlement of the Cape Colony. This all changed in 1866, when a fifteen-year-old Boer called Erasmus Jacobs discovered a diamond on his father's farm. Soon, tens of thousands of British settlers including Cecil Rhodes (see box) were travelling to a town in Cape Colony called Kimberley to mine for diamonds. The economic potential of Cape Colony further increased in 1886, when gold was discovered in Transvaal. The British established an uneasy peace with the Boers, but this peace would not last for long.

Cecil Rhodes

Rhodes arrived in Cape Colony from Britain in 1870 at the age of 17, and invested in the growing diamond mines of Kimberley.

Having become enormously wealthy, Rhodes entered politics. By 1890, Rhodes was Prime Minister of Cape Colony, the founder of the De Beers diamond company, and the director of the British South Africa Company. The Company pioneered British expansion into lands north of Cape Colony searching for more gold, in what are today Zimbabwe and Zambia. The new colony was named 'Rhodesia' after its founder.

Cartoon of Cecil Rhodes standing astride the African continent, 1892

Rhodes embodied Victorian Britain's belief in its national superiority. As a young man, he wrote: "I contend that [the English] are the first race of the world and that the more of the world we inhabit the better it is for the human race". Rhodes dreamt of building an African railroad from Cape Town in the south, to Cairo in the north, which never left British controlled territory.

Check your understanding

1. Why was the Suez Canal such an important part of world trade?

2. How did the British Empire gain informal rule of Egypt from 1882 onwards?

3. What happened at the Battle of Omdurman?

4. Why did the British show more interest in settling Cape Colony after 1866?

5. What role did Cecil Rhodes play in Britain's colonisation of southern Africa?

Ruling the Empire

By the end of the 19th century, the British Empire covered vast swathes of North America, the Caribbean, Africa, South Asia and Australia.

Added to this were a number of smaller colonies, strategically located to spread British power across the globe. These included Cyprus and Gibraltar in the Mediterranean; the Falklands Islands in the South Atlantic; Singapore and **Hong Kong** in the Pacific; and Aden in the Middle East. It was a popular saying that the sun never set on the British Empire.

Trade

By the mid-19th century, Britain produced around half of the world's manufactured goods. The Empire provided guaranteed markets for their export.

Due to Britain's dominance in the world, there were few global conflicts from 1815 to 1914. This period of peace - sometimes called *Pax Britannica* – allowed international trade to grow. The benefits of this trade, however, were not spread equally. Between 1757 and 1947, Britain's gross domestic product per capita increased by 347 percent, but India's increased by only 14 percent.

Britain did invest in the infrastructure of its colonies. By 1900, the British had built 24 000 miles of railway track and 50 000 miles of roads in India. The British also irrigated large parts of India and Egypt, significantly increasing the area of land available to farm. Life expectancy in India increased by eleven years over the period of British rule.

Nevertheless, India suffered repeated famines during British rule. One of the worst began in Bengal in 1769, killing an estimated 10 million people. A century later, the Great Famine struck southern Indian in 1876–78, killing an estimated 5 million people. Both famines were blamed on British policies, such as encouraging Indian farmers to grow **cash crops** for export (tea, **opium**, cotton) at the expense of growing crops for food.

During the 19th century, Britain's merchants imported Indian grown opium to China, in exchange for valuable Chinese goods such as tea and silk. This illegal trade caused widespread opium addiction in China, and Britain conducted it against the wishes of the Chinese Emperor. When China tried to stop Britain importing opium into their country in 1839, it led to the Opium War. Britain defeated China in 1842, gaining control of the Chinese island of Hong Kong.

> ## Fact
>
> The Empire spread British sports such as football, rugby and cricket across the world. In 1882, the Australian cricket team won their first Test match on English soil at the Oval. A British newspaper joked that English cricket had died, been cremated, and the ashes would be taken back to Australia. This joke gave birth to the Ashes cricket series.

Photograph taken during India's Great Famine, 1876

Colonial government

There was no uniform model of government for Britain's colonies. The **settlement colonies** of Australia, New Zealand, Cape Colony and Canada – sometimes called 'dominions' - had the most independence. This was because Britain believed such colonies, inhabited by white settlers, were capable of 'responsible government'. Settlement colonies had their own elected parliaments and governments, which had control over the colony's domestic policy.

The **dependent colonies** were very different. In these colonies, most notably the British Raj, a small class of British officials governed the native population. The Colonial Secretary in London appointed a governor to be in charge of each colony. Within the colony, each province would be ruled by a British Commissioner, and within the province, each district would be ruled by a British District Officer.

The number of British officials, however, remained surprisingly small. By 1900, the Raj had no more than 1000 officials in its civil service, ruling a population of 281 million people. The British made this system work through co-operation with native power structures. African chieftains, Indian maharajas, Arab sheiks, and Malayan sultans could all keep some power over their territories, provided they answered to a British superior.

The army of the British Empire contained troops from many of its colonies. This illustration shows soldiers of the West India Regiment, around 1890

In 1898, the British Army had 116 000 men stationed throughout the Empire, 75 000 of whom were in India. The Royal Navy provided another 100 000 men. Colonies would rarely have felt as if they existed under a military occupation. However, when rebellions did occur, the British Army's response could be brutal.

At the end of the century, the British Empire became involved in one of its most brutal conflicts yet, the Boer War. Britain wanted to expand its power from Cape Colony into the Boer state of the Transvaal, but the tough Boer farmers proved extremely difficult to defeat. Under the command of Lord Kitchener, The British Army destroyed Boer villages, burnt their crops, killed their cattle, and prevented their movement with enormous barbed wire fences. Boer families who had lost their homes were housed in new settlements, which became known as **concentration camps**.

British-built concentration camp, used to house Boers displaced from their homes

Conditions in the concentration camps were dreadful, leading to the deaths of 25 000 Boers, and 12 000 Africans. Britain won the Boer War in 1902, but at great cost to the Empire's reputation at home and abroad.

Check your understanding

1. Why is the period from 1815 to 1914 sometimes known as the *Pax Britannica*?
2. How did the British Empire affect the livelihood of people living in the Raj?
3. How were settlement colonies governed within the British Empire?
4. How were dependent colonies governed within the British Empire?
5. Why did the Boer War cause great damage to the British Empire's reputation?

Unit 6: The Victorian Empire
Knowledge organiser

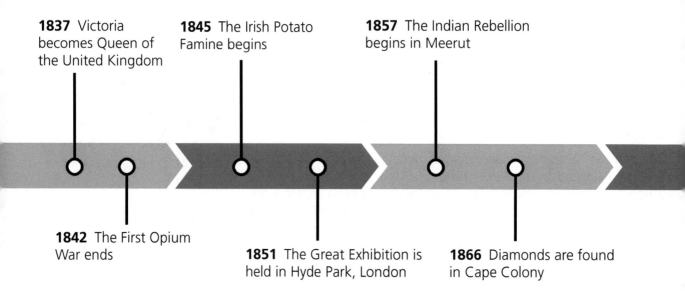

1837 Victoria becomes Queen of the United Kingdom

1845 The Irish Potato Famine begins

1857 The Indian Rebellion begins in Meerut

1842 The First Opium War ends

1851 The Great Exhibition is held in Hyde Park, London

1866 Diamonds are found in Cape Colony

Key vocabulary

Absentee landlord Landowner who does not live nearby and rarely visits the property they let

Boer Descendants of Dutch-speaking settlers in Southern Africa

Cape Colony British colony on the southern tip of the African continent, gained in 1814

Cash crop Crops farmed to be sold commercially, and not for the farmer's own use

Civil service The permanent staff of a government, responsible for administering the country

Concentration camp A camp where a government forces an enemy population to live

Crystal Palace Large iron and glass structure built in Hyde Park in 1851

Dependent colony A colony in which a small number of officials rule a large native population

Great Exhibition International exhibition celebrating industry and culture held in 1851

Home Rule Policy advocating that Ireland regains its own government, and own Parliament

Hong Kong Island to the south of mainland China, ceded to Britain in 1842

Irish Republican Brotherhood Secret organisation formed by Irish nationalists

Maharajas Indian Princes who ruled their states in partnership with the British Empire

Maxim gun The world's first recoil operated machine gun

Missionary A person sent to spread their religion to others, particularly in a foreign country

Mutiny Rebellion against authority, often soldiers or sailors against their commanding officers

Omdurman Site of battle in the Sudan, which showed superiority of European firepower

Opium Highly addictive drug, obtained from the juice of the poppy seed

Pax Britannica Long period of international peace, overseen by the British Empire

Puppet government Situation where a country's ruler is controlled by an outside power

Raj Term for British ruled India from 1858 until Indian Independence in 1947

Sepoy An Indian soldier serving in the British Indian Army

1876 Queen Victoria becomes Empress of India

1898 British victory at the Battle of Omdurman

1882 British Army occupies Egypt

1899 The start of the Boer War

1901 Death of Queen Victoria

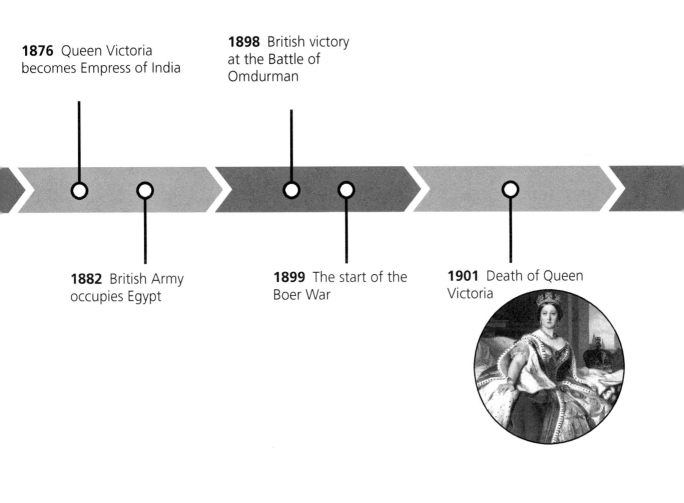

Key vocabulary

Settlement colony Colony in which native population is outnumbered by foreign arrivals

Suez Canal Man-made shipping route, connecting Mediterranean Ocean with India Ocean

Sutti The Hindu custom of widows throwing themselves on their husband's funeral pyre

Tenant Someone who occupies land or property rented from a landlord

Transvaal Independent Boer republic which existed until 1902 in southern Africa

Key people

Cecil Rhodes Businessman and politician in southern Africa, and keen supporter of Empire

Florence Nightingale Army nurse who became a celebrated national figure due to her work in the Crimea

Lord Bentinck Governor General of India from 1828, who wanted to reform Indian society

Lord Kitchener British Field Marshall, and commander during the Boer War

Prince Albert German husband to Queen Victoria, helped organise the Great Exhibition

Queen Victoria Queen who ruled Britain at the height of its Empire's power

Index

navvies 49, 51, 52
nawabs 8–9, 16
Nelson, Horatio 37, 41
New York 20–1, 51
Newcomen, Thomas 42–3, 52
Nightingale, Florence 67, 77

Omdurman, battle of 72, 76–7
Opium Wars 74, 76
overcrowding 54–5

Paine, Thomas 36, 41
Paris, treaty of 13, 17
Parliament 10–11, 18, 21, 26, 29, 55, 59, 61, 63, 64–5, 70–1
Pasha, Tewfik 72
patriotism 15, 16
Pax Britannica 74, 76
peasants 30, 32
Peel, Robert 62, 63, 65
penal colonies 10–11, 16
People's Charter 61, 65
Peterloo Massacre 60, 64
philanthropy 63, 64
Pilgrim Fathers 6, 17
Pitt, Thomas 8, 17
Pitt, William, the Elder 15, 17
Pitt, William, the Younger 36
plantations 6, 7, 22, 26, 28
Plassey, battle of 9, 12, 16
polarisation 32–3, 40
police 62–3, 64
political reform 60–1
Poor Law Amendments 59, 64
poverty 30, 54–5, 59, 70
press gangs 13, 17
prison reforms 63
propaganda 35
Protestants 70, 73
Prussia 32–3, 35, 38–40
public health 55, 65
Puritans 6

Quebec 12, 17, 20
Quiberon Bay, battle of 13, 17

racial superiority 67
radicals 30, 32, 35–6, 40, 60–1, 70
railways 48–9, 50–1, 53
'Raj' 69, 75, 76
Reibey, Mary 11
Revolutionary Army 33, 34
Rhodes, Cecil 73, 77
Roanoke 6
Robespierre, Max 33–4, 41
rookeries 62, 64
rotten boroughs 60, 64
Royal African Company 22, 28
Royal Charters 6, 7, 8, 16
Royal Navy 10, 12–13, 27, 37, 47, 75
Russia 38–9, 41

St Helena 39, 41
Sancho, Ignatius 27, 29
sans-culottes 33, 41
Saratoga 20–1, 28, 29
'scorched earth' campaigns 38, 41
Scotland 15
scurvy 13, 17, 37
seamen 12–13
settlement 6–7, 10–11
Seven Years' War 12–13, 15–18, 20, 47
sewers 55
Slave Trade Act 1807 27, 29
slavery 7, 15, 21–7, 29
Slavery Abolition Act 27, 29
social reform 58–9
Spain 7, 11, 16, 22, 35, 37
spinning 42–4, 52
spinning jenny 44, 52, 53
sport 74
Stamp Act 18, 28, 29
steam engine 42–7, 52–3
steam trains 48–51, 53, 66
steamships 51, 53, 67
Stephenson, George 49, 50, 53
Sudan 72
Suez Canal 72, 77
sugar 7, 14, 22, 24, 26

Tasmania 11
taxation 9, 15, 18, 30–1, 34
tea 14, 19

telegrams 51
Terror, The 33, 35, 41
textiles 14, 44–5, 56–7, 58
Third Reform Act 61, 65
thirteen colonies 18–20
tobacco 6–7, 14, 15, 22, 24
Tolpuddle Martyrs 58–9, 64–5
Tone, Wolfe 36, 41
trade 8, 12, 14–15, 22–3, 38, 74
Trafalgar, battle of 37, 40
transport 48–51, 67
Transvaal 73, 75, 77
Trevithick, Richard 48–9, 53
triangular trade 22, 29

ud-Daulah, Siraj 9
unions 58, 65
United Irishmen 36, 40, 70
United Kingdom 36, 41, 70
United States 19–21, 51, 71
urbanisation 54–5, 62, 65

Versailles 31, 32, 41
Victoria 4, 66–7, 69, 76–7
Virginia 6, 17, 21, 23, 24
Virginia Company 6, 16
vote 60–1

Washington, George 20–1, 29, 30
Waterloo, battle of 39–41
Watt, James 42–5, 47, 52–3
wealth 13, 14–15, 23
weaving 44, 53
Wedgewood, Josiah 26
Wellington, Duke of 38–9, 41
West Indies 26, 27, 29
White, John 6
Wilberforce, William 26–7, 29
Wilkinson, John 47, 53
windmills 42
Wolfe, General 12, 17
Wollstonecraft, Mary 36, 41
wool, merino 11
workers' rights 58–9
workhouses 59, 65
working classes 61, 65

Acknowledgements

Thank you to all the friends, family, colleagues and former teachers who helped me to write this book. More people than I could mention have given up their time to read early drafts, fact check certain sections, and offer advice. I am hugely grateful for the generosity of you all.

Robert Peal

Every effort has been made to trace copyright holders and to obtain their permission for use of copyright material. The publishers will gladly receive any information enabling them to rectify any error or omission at first opportunity. The publishers would like to thank the following for permission to reproduce copyright material:

(t = top, b = bottom, c = centre, l = left, r = right)

Cover & p1 typografie/Alamy; p6 Mary Evans Picture Library/Alamy; p7t North Wind Picture Archives/Alamy; p7b Danita Delimont/Alamy; p8t aravind chandramohanan/Alamy; p8b World History Archive/Alamy; p9b Pjr Tra\vel/Alamy; p9t Granger Historical Picture Archive; p10t G L Archive/Alamy; p10b Pictorial Press Ltd/Alamy; p11 Travel Pictures/Alamy; p12t INTERFOTO/Alamy; p12b Liquid Light/Alamy; p13 Florilegius/alamy; p14t Geffrye Museum/Alamy; p14b The Archives/Alamy; p15t Heritage Image Partnership Ltd/Alamy; p15b Sam Toren/Alamy; p17 G L Archive/Alamy; p18 Pictorial Press Ltd/Alamy; p19t Niday Picture Library/Alamy; p19b G l Archive/Alamy; p20 Joe Vogan/Alamy; p21t North Wind Pictures; p21b Taharch/Shutterstock; p22t Gary Cook/Alamy; p22b Granger Historical Picture Archive/Alamy; p23 World History Archive/Alamy; p24 Lordprice Collection/Alamy; p25 Universal Images Group North America LLC/Alamy; p26t&b Granger Historical Archive/Alamy; p27t G L Archive; 27b Mary Evans Picture Library/alamy; p29 Granger Historical Picture Archive/Alamy; p30t G L Archive/Alamy; p30b Josse Christophel/Alamy; p31 SuperStock/Alamy; p32 Josse Christophel/Alamy; p33 Niday Picture Library/Alamy; p34t G L Archive/Alamy; p34c Pictorial Press Ltd/Alamy; p34b Atlaspix/Alamy; p35r G L Archive/Alamy; p35l Artepics/Alamy; p36t Mary Evans Picture Library/Alamy; p36b Holmes Garden Photo/Alamy; p37 Ian Dagnall; p38t G L Archive; p38b Alexander Tolstykh/Shutterstock; p39t Lifestyle Pictures/Alamy; p39b Gillian Moore/Alamy; p41 Artepics/Alamy; p42t Craig Joiner Photography/Alamy; p42b Digital Image Library; p42c Chronicle/Alamy; p43 Granger Historical Picture Archive/Alamy; p44t Andrew Roland/Alamy; p44b Photo Researchers Inc/Alamy; p45t World History Archive/Alamy; p46t North Wind Picture Archives/Alamy; p46b V&A Images/Alamy; p47t World History Archive/Alamy; p47b eye35.pix/Alamy; p48t The Keasbury-Gordon Collection/Alamy; p48b Glasshouse Images/Alamy; p49t Graham Oliver/Alamy; p49b Wolverhampton Archives/Alamy; p50t World History Archive/Alamy; p50b Peter Barritt/Alamy; p51 Heritage Image Partnership/Alamy; pp54t&b, p55 Pictorial Press Ltd/Alamy; p56 Pictorial Press Ltd/Alamy; p57t The Print Collector/Alamy; p57b Mary Evans Picture Library/Alamy; p58 Pictorial Press Ltd/Alamy; p59t Mary Evans Picture Library/Alamy; p59b Pictorial Press Ltd/Alamy; p60t Pictorial Press Ltd; p60b Digital Image Library/Alamy; p61t Chronicle/Alamy; p61b Lordprice Collection/Alamy; p62 G L Archive/Alamy; p63 World History Archive/Alamy; p66t Lordprice Collection/Alamy; p66b G L Archive; p67 Lebrecht Music and Arts Photo Library/Alamy; p68t Dinodia Photos/Alamy; p68b Pictorial Press Ltd/Alamy; p69 Classic Image/Alamy; p70t david hancock/Alamy; p70b Granger Historial Pictire Archive/Alamy; p71 Classic Image/Alamy; p72t Arco Images GmbH/Alamy; p72b Lebrecht Music and Arts Photo Library/Alamy; p73t North Wind Picture Archives/Alamy; p73b Granger Historical Picture Archive/Alamy; p74 Antiqua Print Gallery/Alamy; p75t INTERFOTO/Alamy; p75b World History Archive/Alamy; p77 Lordprice Collection/Alamy.

SUFFOLK LACE

and
the Lacemakers of Eye

Nicky Höwener-Townsend

First published in the UK 2009 by
Nicky Höwener-Townsend,
Seahaven, 7 Beaconsfield Road, Kessingland, Suffolk. NR33 7RD

ISBN 978-0-9563018-0-2

Printed and bound by Leiston Press

In memory of

Jessie Caunt

a founder member
of
Suffolk Lacemakers

CONTENTS

FOREWORD

A well researched and fascinating account of little known Suffolk lace, this is a welcome addition to our knowledge of English lace. A clear, concise and well documented account, achieved by Nicky's determination and effort, from a wide range of sources allows the reader to accompany her on this quest for information. The book has wide interest, not only for the lace enthusiast but also as a historical document giving proof of a cottage industry in Eye. It will offer ideas and encouragement to anyone considering a similar project.

The collection of patterns, many with designs not seen elsewhere, provides an interesting alternative for those who enjoy straightforward point ground edgings. The author has studied the original work and prepared prickings and working diagrams to ensure that the lace is made exactly as the samples found in the museum - her determination for accuracy is admirable - as she notes that stitches do not necessarily conform to normal practice.

The clarity of the prickings and diagrams with the clear photographs of well made lace ensure that Suffolk Lace is a welcome addition to our collection of English point ground lace.

Pamela Nottingham
2009

ACKNOWLEDGEMENTS

This book has been several years in the making and there were moments when I wondered if it would ever come to fruition, so thank you to all those members of today's Suffolk Lacemakers, especially Karin Wheals and Carol Lewis, who have encouraged, helped and supported me throughout this venture. My thanks also to Pam Nottingham for her knowledge and expertise, to Jacqui Barber and Carol McFadzean for their encouragement and advice, to Gilly Blachford, Pat Hansford, Carol Lewis and Pam Lugg for their invaluable contribution in reworking the lace samples, from which I have learnt so much and not forgetting Richard Ives who turned his bobbin making skills to producing a wonderful set of replica Suffolk bobbins for me.

I would also like to extend my thanks to the staff at the various museums and repositories I have visited during the course of my research, for the assistance given, in particular to Joan Lyall of Ipswich Museum: Mei Boatman of Colchester Museum: Shelley Tobin and Natalie Raw at the Royal Albert Memorial Museum, Exeter: Ros Watson at the Royal Pump Room Museum, Harrogate: Rachel Silverson of Northampton Museum: Kate Hay, Catherine Flood, Oliver Winchester, Esther Ketskemety and Antonia Brodie of the V&A Museum, London: Inger Lauridsen of Museum Sønderjylland, Tønder, Denmark: Myra Stanbury and Ray Coffee of the Western Australia Museum also the Salisbury & Wiltshire Museum and Diss Museum, Norfolk and Steve Penny of the Diss Express.

My thanks to the numerous repositories where information was sought, Suffolk Record Office, in particular Ivan Bunn at Lowestoft: Don, Pam, Mary, Elaine and Mark at the LDS Family History Centre, Lowestoft: Centre for Kentish Studies, Maidstone: Northampton Record Office: Westminster City Archive: Guildhall Library London: and the London Metropolitan Archives.

Thanks must also go to Doug Baker, Margaret Buttle, Geoff Caulton, Margaret Dorrell, Albert & Eileen Frost, Faith Legg, Brian Lemin, Joan Maynard, Carole Morris, Pompi Parry, Jan Perry, Scilla Stephenson, Dr. Phyllis Wells and Jeanette Williams for sharing their knowledge and information; Ruth Budge and Jean Nathan for their help with computer issues. My appreciation to Ivan Bunn, Alan & Carol Lewis, Jim Ringrose and John & Karin Wheals, for proof reading and suggesting improvements to the manuscript and to Carol Maxwell for preparing the index.

Thank you to those who have granted permission for the inclusion of photographs and articles in the book. While every effort has been made to trace and acknowledge all copyright holders, I would like to apologise should there be any errors or omissions.

Most importantly though I would also like to thank my husband Brian, for his invaluable help with the photography and without whose unfailing support and encouragement this book would not have become a reality.

The Lacemaker

Her fingers move with infinite skill
And pins their plan reveal;
Till the work appears on its cushioned hill
As a tiny forest of steel,
Where threads all gather in intricate pools
Which the pin-trees shade from sight,
And over-spill to their bobbin-spools
In thin clear streams of white.

Her fingers decide with infinite skill
The path that each thread takes;
And it all seems very peaceful until
One of the threads defies her will
And ups and goes and breaks!

by Gerald Lovell

Introduction

Although not Suffolk born and bred, I have lived in the county for most of my life and when I began to make lace, back in the late 1980's, I certainly hadn't envisaged writing a book on the subject. At the time, I have to confess, I was far more interested in actually making lace rather than studying its history. However, having become acquainted with the laces of Honiton, Bedfordshire and Buckinghamshire, a natural curiosity lead me to ponder about Suffolk's past and so I would look through books on the subject to see if any such reference might be found between their covers; after all it didn't hurt to dream!

It was whilst browsing through Palliser's *History of Lace*[1] that I came across my first reference to Suffolk in connection with lace. Here was a picture of four pieces of lace to be found in the Victoria and Albert Museum, but my spirits were slightly dampened when I read the entry, for it stated that Suffolk produced laces *"of little artistic value"*. Other references gradually came to my attention, but they were mostly sourced from Palliser and added little information.

Time passed and I came across a copy of Pat Earnshaw's *A Dictionary of Lace*,[2] but it only served to dampen my spirits further when I read the entry headed 'Suffolk Lace'. It briefly detailed the history of a commercial lace school in Malmesbury which saw a revival in 1907 under the patronage of the Countess of Suffolk. Joan Blanchard also gives an account of this in her book on Malmesbury Lace.[3] Earnshaw then explains that because of this patronage, Malmesbury lace was sometimes known as 'Suffolk' lace. The lace is described as being similar to that of nearby Downton and laces made in the East Midlands. The reader is then referred to the illustrations of Suffolk lace depicted in Palliser, comparing them to examples of Downton lace shown in Salisbury Museum's handbook. The implication being, that the Suffolk lace depicted in Palliser was therefore, a product of the Malmesbury industry listed under its pseudonym. It was a disappointing read, for it now seemed that lace had not been produced in the county of Suffolk after all.

Some twenty years later, having given scant thought to the subject, I made a chance discovery and this book is the result. It is an opportunity to set the record straight, and record as much of the remaining evidence of Suffolk's overlooked and forgotten lacemaking past, making available to today's lacemakers, be they from Suffolk or elsewhere, those patterns that were once so readily dismissed as being of little artistic value.

A Chance Discovery

Christmas 2000 was fast approaching and I had been shopping for a present for my husband, in a small collectables shop in Beccles, a small town on the Suffolk/ Norfolk border. Having made my purchase I happened to ask if they might have anything that was lace related. The lady scurried off to the back room for a few minutes to search her stock and soon returned with a postcard. It depicted a 90 year old lady sitting outside a cottage door, with a lace pillow before her and a bobbin winder to her side. At first glance it was similar to many other postcards of this genre, but closer inspection quickly revealed what made this one special; for the words printed across the bottom read –:

'A Suffolk Lace Maker, aged 90 years, with antique bobbin winder. Sold in aid of the Universities' Mission to Central Africa'.

Barely able to believe what I was seeing and trying desperately to contain my excitement, I handed over £1.50 for the postcard and departed, tightly clutching my purchases and headed for home. The drive home seemed to take an age; my poor head was spinning in a whirl of excitement, I so desperately wanted to share this amazing find with my husband and then I suddenly realised that I couldn't, it was going to have to remain a secret until after Christmas!

Christmas Day came and went, the postcard had all but slipped from my mind when my husband asked if I would proof read the quarterly newsletter for Suffolk Lacemakers. The group was officially formed in 1984 to promote lacemaking in the county and he was editor. Upon reaching page three I could scarcely believe what I was reading, the coincidence rendered me almost speechless. The article entitled 'Suffolk Lace' was written by Jessie Caunt, one of the group's founding members. I rushed upstairs to retrieve my secret postcard, for in the article, Jessie referred to one depicting a 90 year old Suffolk lacemaker, and described the very postcard I was by now holding in my rather shaky hands.

Needless to say a coherent explanation was eventually given to my slightly bemused husband, who was just a touch perplexed at all the fuss. The February newsletter duly went to print with a picture of my postcard alongside Jessie's article.

Jessie Caunt's Article

The following article, was first published in Suffolk Lacemakers newsletter in February 2001, and is reproduced with permission.

* * * * *

Little is known about Suffolk as a lace making area, except that lace made in the county was similar to Bucks Point.

In 1978 new light was thrown on this once flourishing cottage industry. During the renovation of the 17th century Dove House in Eye, two lace bobbins had been found in the ceiling space. They were of the Flemish type with a single neck and bulbous end. Soon after this the Mayor of Eye told of a find of five bobbins in the ceiling of his home [Pocky House] during renovation. Then a postcard turned up showing an elderly lady seated at a lace pillow using bulbous ended bobbins. Beneath the picture is printed 'A Suffolk Lace Maker - aged 90 years'.

A local historian and journalist published the story of the postcard and bobbins in the local press to coincide with an exhibition in Eye Church, where the postcard and bobbins formed a small exhibit.

Following this, more evidence of Eye's lacemaking past turned up, a bobbin from Mr Maynard, the chemist, found in the ceiling; a bobbin from beneath the staircase in Bob Cotton's cottage at Yaxley. The lacemaker was recognised as Mary 'Polly' Collins of Yaxley by a relative. Another relative sent a yard of lace which she had watched her great aunt make.

The only other known examples of Suffolk Lace are in the Victoria and Albert Museum. There are about 50 bobbins from seven separate sources, also a bobbin winder and some prickings.

The Suffolk lace industry seems to have developed independently from the main lace areas, and died earlier, due probably to its simple designs. The centre was almost certainly Eye. The distinct Suffolk bobbin shape would indicate its origins as probably being the same Flemish refugees who brought their weaving skills to East Anglia.

* * * * *

1. SUFFOLK LACE

Where is Eye?

Suffolk forms the southern half of the bulge that makes up East Anglia. It is bounded by Norfolk to the north, Essex to the south and Cambridgeshire to the west, while its eastern shores are lapped by the North Sea.

Eye, which is where some of the bobbins had been found, lies roughly midway, but slightly south of, the Norfolk/Suffolk border and just east of the A140, the main Ipswich to Norwich road.

Its name, once spelt Aye, comes from the Old English meaning island[4], for it is almost, though perhaps not quite so obviously, surrounded by water. The River Dove flows around the town to its south and south east, while a stream from the nearby village of Yaxley flows to its north to meet the Dove. Marshland, known locally as the Town Moor, lies to the south and west.

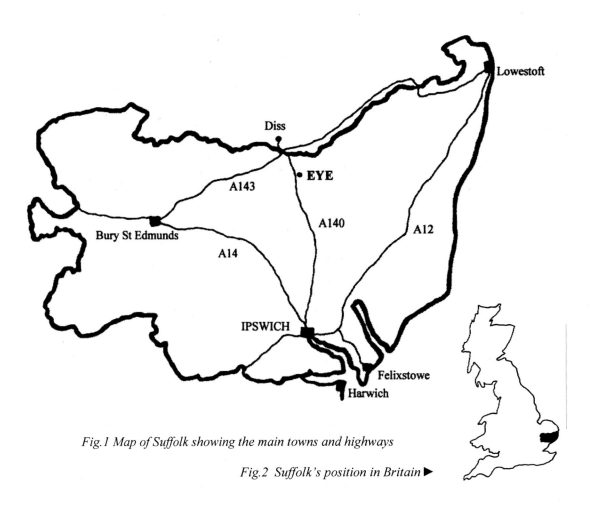

Fig.1 Map of Suffolk showing the main towns and highways

Fig.2 Suffolk's position in Britain ▶

Back in 1738 the town was described as "a borough-town, by some called the Island, because it is surrounded by a brook; its market is weekly on Saturday; it has one large handsome church, and is governed by two bailiffs and a common council, and sends two members to parliament."[5] Eye was once a market town of some significance and importance, but fortunes changed and it gradually became overshadowed by nearby Diss.

Today, Eye is a quiet and unassuming town that nestles quietly in the Waveney Valley, basking in its distinctive rural charm. Its market has gone, but its handsome 14th century church remains a key landmark on the town's skyline. Robert Malet's Castle built in the days after the Conquest and now a ruin, straddles the Motte watching over the town. The striking half timbered Guildhall dating from the 15th century, housed the town's Grammar School for many years.

Fig.3 Also known as Magdalen Street these cottages were home to many of Eye's lacemakers, the cottages on the left were demolished in 1921

Gleanings from local newspapers

It was in 1981, when the first two bobbins were found in Eye during renovation work on a restaurant, then known as Dove House. A further group of similar bobbins was also discovered, again in Eye and during renovation work on a cottage that was once the town's "Pest House" or "Pocky House". Also at this time a postcard, identical to the one that I was to purchase later, came into the possession of Faith Legg, who ran a bookshop in the town.

This led to local journalist and historian, Mike Burrows, writing an article which was published in the East Anglian Daily Times on 25th June 1981, including a picture of the postcard. More information came to light and a follow-up article was printed in October 1981.

Under floor treasures found in village pub

BURIED treasures from hundreds of years ago have been discovered during alterations to a village pub.

Roy and Margaret Buttle, who run the Bull at Yaxley, uncovered dozens of everyday items from the past when they began moving the bar in the pub, which celebrates its 400th birthday in 1992.

A child's shoe, coins, medals, bobbins and musket balls emerged into the daylight at the weekend for the first time since they disappeared down gaps and cracks in the ancient pub. "There were some beams across one of the rooms and we wanted to discover if they held anything up," Margaret explained.

So the Buttles and some of their regular customers set-to and pulled up floorboards in the room above, exposing wooden fluted beams. Eager to investigate further, they began lifting floorboards and pulling down ceilings everywhere — uncovering dozens of lost and forgotten items.

"We all had a ripping time. It was fantastic. We were all scrabbling around and one of the people had a metal detector," said Margaret.

A tiny slipper, bobbins with cotton still wound around them, cartwheel pennies from the 1700s, Victorian commemorative medals, a silver St George coin and a hat pin bearing the RAF crest, were just some of the finds.

The Buttles, who have been running the free house for almost two years, plan to find out more about their treasures from an expert and hope eventually to mount them in a display case at the pub.

Fig.4 A report of the bobbin find at "The Bull" Yaxley
Reproduced by courtesy of the Diss Express and Margaret Buttle

Mike Burrows had received a letter from a Mrs. Margaret Cooper, who identified the lacemaker in the postcard as Miss Mary Collins, a relation on her mother's side, and she had enclosed another earlier photograph of Mary sitting outside the same cottage, making lace. A second letter had been received from Mrs. Bessie Copping, who also identified the lacemaker as Mary Collins, and recalled that everyone in her family had always called her great aunt "Polly". She recounted having watched Mary making a lace edging and being given the strip of lace as a gift.

Mrs. Margaret Buttle with the discovered items at Yaxley Bull.

Fig.5 Reproduced by courtesy of the Diss Express and Margaret Buttle

Two further local newspaper cuttings from the Diss Express, during March 1988, recounted the events at The Bull Inn, Yaxley, (now called The Auberge). Roy and Margaret Buttle were undertaking some renovation work to the pub, this led to an old plaster ceiling being taken down and dozens of lost and forgotten items were found. Coins dating from 1797 to 1817, hundreds of buttons, musket balls, a baby's leather shoe, medals, pieces of clay pipes and five wooden bobbins.

Margaret later told me that a display case had been mounted onto a wall in the bar to exhibit the treasures found at the pub.

One rather surprising, and much earlier, article came to light while searching through film indexes for the Ipswich Journal at the county's Record Office; but for this index it would probably have remained buried amongst the tiny print of the day.

Dated 10 February 1821 it read under the heading **"Shopkeepers buying lace without licence."** During the previous week *"two men and a woman, supposed from Eye"* had been travelling *"about the parishes of Walton and Kirton [near Felixstowe] selling British Lace"*. They had apparently become concerned about a number of *"shopkeepers and others who sell that article without having obtained a licence for that purpose"*, and had clearly reported this wrong doing, hence the article with the added warning *"We publish this as a caution to the trade to be on their guard against such persons"*.[6]

Establishing the Industry's Presence

The earliest written reference to lacemaking in Eye that I have found so far was in Richard Blome's Britannia, published in 1673, he wrote that *"The womens employ in this Town is making of Bone-lace"*.[7] Some 57 years later the Magna Britannia published in 1730 also refers to the women of Eye who *"employ themselves chiefly in making Bone-lace"*.[8] While in The New General English Dictionary circa.1738, there are two entries, one for Aye the other under Eye. Both record that it is *"the women [who] are employed in [the] making [of] bone-lace,"* which is the town's *"principle manufacture"*.[9] Moving on by some 80 years Samuel Pinnock tells us that in 1818 many of Eye's 1,893 inhabitants *"are employed in the manufacture of bone-lace"*[10] a sentiment repeated a few years later by John Kirby in 1829.[11] Pigot's Directories of 1830[12] and 1839[13] are both a little more specific as to the type of women making lace, for they are recorded as being, *"of the humbler class of industrious females"*. The ratio of women involved in making lace must have been proportionally high in relation to the population for these writers to feel it worthy of mention.

Fig.6 Lambseth Street, Eye

Unlike the census of 1841 which lists just a few women as lace weavers, that of 1851 paints a rather different picture. For even though the industry was by now moving towards a decline, there are 174 lace weavers recorded within a five mile radius of Eye.

However, just seven years later the industry was now being referred to in the past tense as Kelly's Directory declared that *"A good trade was carried on in this town some years ago in the making of pillow lace, which gave employment to the wives and children of the agricultural labourers; but since the introduction of machinery it has become nearly extinct"*.[14] Morris's Directory of 1868 continued in the same vein, again claiming that the town's declining lace trade was due to the *"introduction of machinery"*.[15]

What had once been an industry of economic importance to the town and its surrounding villages, lace had after all been described as the town's "principal manufacture", had fallen into a very rapid decline. The Census of 1861 supports this, for only 28 lace weavers and 4 former lace weavers are recorded within that same five mile radius of Eye.

Over a period ranging from between 1837 and 1861 I discovered the names of 229 lacemakers and they were the industry's remnant. We shall probably never know the full extent of the industry or just how many women and children, or even men, were actually involved in making this delicate and beautiful textile but what we do know is that they had at least 180 years of lacemaking history behind them.

What is Suffolk lace?

To try and answer this question, I began by returning to study the few brief entries to be found in the various books on the subject. The first reference to Suffolk lace, in Mrs Bury Palliser's History of Lace, doesn't appear until the book's 4th edition, published in 1902. This particular edition was in fact jointly revised after Mrs Palliser's death in 1878, by Margaret Jourdain and Alice Dryden. Palliser attributes most of the Suffolk lace designs as being *"derived from simple Mechlin, Lille and Valencienne patterns"*.[16] Mechlin, Lille and Valencienne lace are generally classed as Flemish laces, despite the turbulent times which saw borders and sovereignty changing. Lille had been the capital of Flanders until the treaty of 1668 when it became French, but its style of lace maintained a strong Flemish influence. While Valencienne, captured by Louis XIV in 1656, was also finally ceded to France in 1678. Penderel Moody is of similar opinion to Palliser, maintaining that *"the Trolly lace of Devon and Suffolk was very similar, in both cases keeping closely to the same Flemish origin"*.[17] Palliser continues that Suffolk produced lace of *"little artistic value…the entire collection displays varied combinations of six ways of plaiting and twisting threads."*[18] However, it also said, the lace resembled that made in Buckinghamshire and Normandy and the samples depicted in plate LXXXVII[19] bore this out. For her own book, entitled Old Lace, Margaret Jourdain simply reiterates the entry from the 4th edition of Palliser adding that *"other [Downton] patterns are exactly like those illustrated as characteristic of Suffolk,"* and that the *"mesh is very large and open; a coarse outlining thread is used to give definition to the simple pattern"*.[20]

Both Thomas Wright[21] and Mrs Nevill Jackson also sourced their information, regarding Suffolk lace, from Palliser, but Jackson includes Jourdain's description of the threads used being *"of varying thickness, coarser threads being frequently used to outline the pattern"*[22] and includes a picture of the plate first depicted in Palliser's 4th edition. However, it must be remembered that what was then described as coarse thread, would by our standards today, be regarded by many and especially to the unknowing eye, as relatively fine.

In The Lace and Embroidery Collector, a guide by Mrs R.E. Head it states that the *"réseaux"* of Suffolk lace *"was more open......and the quality generally inferior"*.[23] While the much later, Romance of Lace by Mary Eirwen Jones adds that the varying thickness of the threads caused *"a shadow effect"* and goes on to describe the techniques used as *"traditional"*.[24] Both Jackson and Eirwen Jones add that Suffolk lace was *"of the peasant Torchon variety"*,[25] but Eirwen Jones has clearly sourced her information from Jackson, whose own source is unclear.

Meanwhile Head also makes mention of *"a coarse lace of coloured worsted, made with very large wooden bobbins"*[26] as being produced in the county; again the source of this information is unclear and I have found no further mention of this lace in Suffolk.

The first more positive and explanatory references to Suffolk lace that emerged, were passed on to me by Carol McFadzean, who came across them in Penderel Moody's books, while researching for her book on Devon Trolly Lace. According to Penderel Moody *"the Midlands were especially famous for it [Trolly lace], but Suffolk, Dorset and Wiltshire, produced equally dainty little edgings, each county showing a certain individuality in treatment"*.[27] She says the name Trolly is of Flemish origin and describes it as a lace worked as a single continuous piece on the round, the pattern encircling the lace pillow, unlike the lace of Honiton and Brussels which is worked in sprigs.[28] According to Mary Sharpe in Pillow and Point Lace the word Trolly was used in some areas to describe the coarse outlining thread[29] while Hudson Moore says the term Trolly Lace was given to *"a class of [English] laces with grounds which resemble the Flemish Trolle Kant grounds, and which have a thick thread cordonnet"*.[30] Penderel Moody also says that the *"peasant laces all belong to the Trolly class"* and that they tended to be *"made in closely recurring repeats like the Torchon"* they could also be worked in quantity by *"peasant workers who would be unequal to making lace which required the exercise of artistic judgement"*.[31] It would also explain why Eirwen Jones described Suffolk lace as being of the *'peasant variety'*.[32]

Penderel Moody attributes the similarity between the Trolly lace of Devon and Suffolk, from having remained true to their origins and describes the patterns' decoration as consisting *"of rings outlined with a heavy gimp thread, and the lace [taking] its name from the number of rings or holes"*. She goes on to say that it was the narrower Trolly laces, often traded by pedlars, that became known as *"Baby laces"*[33] to distinguish them from the wider and more costly Trolly laces, and three such edgings, very similar to Suffolk patterns, are depicted in Plate II of Penderel Moody's book.[34]

The four lace samples pictured in Palliser (see picture opposite), were all notably different in design but were clearly what Penderel Moody described as Trolly laces. The first sample reminded me of a Danish Tønder pattern, with its simple pattern and deeply pointed scallops, that had been influenced by the French Empire Style of the early 19th century and it suits Moody's description with the thick thread outlining rings. The second design, an insertion, was created by a thick meandering gimp thread through a net ground, enclosing a central area worked in honeycomb stitch, simple but quite effective. The pattern of the third sample was more involved but again set within a net ground sprinkled with a few tallies. Gimp work created the outline of the design which contained short cloth stitch trails, honeycomb rings and areas of honeycomb with a mayflower. Notably, it was the only sample with picots. The fourth edging pictured is best described as comprising a honeycomb ground, set with cloth stitch diamonds and a slightly unusual style of fan, worked in thread more usually associated with gimp work.

Fig.7 Reproduction of Plate LXXXVII *from Palliser's "History of Lace"*
using samples redrawn and worked by the author

The Origins of the Suffolk Industry

Quite how lacemaking came to Suffolk and became established in Eye is unclear. We know from Blome, that Eye's lacemakers were industriously working at their pillows in 1673, and significantly, it was the only industry or trade that he mentioned for the town, which does seem to emphasis its importance for the local economy and in turn, suggests that it had been established some years beforehand. However, information pre-dating Blome has come to light and it reveals that lace was being made in Suffolk as early as 1597.

The document from which this information comes, records a Census of the Poor taken in Ipswich during the reign of Elizabeth I, evidence suggests it dates from October 1597. Its purpose was to enable local officials, to devise an effective way of administering relief to those affected by poverty and what remains of the census, covers nine of the town's parishes. The original document is held in the Ipswich Borough archives, but a transcription was made by John Webb for the Suffolk Records Society.[35]

Amongst those recorded in the table for the parish of St. Stephen's is a young widow. She is just 27 years old with three young children. The oldest child, a girl, for it says that *"She goeth to knitting schole,"* and two children of 3 and 2½ years. However, it is what the census records about the children's mother that is so significant for it reads, *"Elizabeth Grimstoune, She maketh boane lace".*[36]

The term 'bone lace' leaves us in no doubt that Elizabeth was making bobbin lace. Palliser explains that the origin of this term was claimed by Fuller in his Worthies of England, to come from the use of sheep's trotters prior to the invention of bobbins.[37] Hudson Moore says that small bones from the trotter or foot were used.[38] Both conjure an interesting image, though of course animal leg bones came to be used by bobbin makers for turning bobbins. Palliser also adds that shaped fish bones were used by many lacemakers because metal pins were more costly.[39]

Having been widowed Elizabeth had become unable to support her young family and they found themselves recipients of the Tooley Foundation. Established through the benefice of Henry Tooley, one of Ipswich's richest merchants in 1551, money was later used from Tooley's bequest to enable the town to purchase Blackfriars and in 1572 Christ's Hospital was established, by Royal Charter.[40] This establishment provided free accommodation, when vacancies occurred, for *"the poor inhabitants of Ipswich and those unable to live without help".*[41] Inmates were required to wear a red and blue badge, possibly with the initials TF and were expected to work, both *"necessarie household service"* to keep the establishment clean and *"honest employment"* to *"both maintain themselves and be compelled to be useful to the Community".*[42] The records show that Elizabeth received relief payments from the Foundation for *"10 we[kes] at 6d and 43 at 12d"* a total of *"£2. 8s. 0d",* [43] though it is unclear as to whether they became inmates or not.

Children benefited from a basic education which included learning skills to aid them in later life, while the Foundation also provided the adults with the necessary tools and materials for employment, doing such things as carding, spinning and weaving. The Foundation clearly encouraged gainful employment and so, although in receipt of relief, Elizabeth would have been permitted to continue working for the local lace dealer. To date I have been unable to discover any information about Elizabeth's husband or his trade and I have found no further mention of either Elizabeth or her children.

While this document doesn't make any clearer how lacemaking came to Suffolk and eventually came to be established in and around Eye, it does confirm that lacemaking had a presence in the county much earlier than previously believed.

Fig.8 Ipswich. The Quay, 1825

The Tudor age was a very fashion conscious time which greatly benefited the lace trade, and it was against this background that the making of bobbin lace in England had begun to emerge in Bedfordshire and Devon, and it seems that this may well have been the case in Suffolk too, for Santina Levey describes lacemaking in England as being *"well established by 1600"*.[44] Ipswich was a major port and not too far removed from Eye, with established and thriving trade routes to the Low Countries. Suffolk's wealth came from the county's wool trade and goods from these centres were being exported to the continent from Ipswich. By 1580, 78% of the region's exported goods by value, was in the form of woollen cloth and most of the skills that came to East Anglia came via the Flemish weavers.[45] Hudson Moore records that *"the commerce between England and the Low Countries was immense"*[46] and John Yallop reminds us that during the latter part of the sixteenth century England *"saw the beginning of a great expansion of the production of consumer goods."* [47]

In his History of the Honiton Lace Industry, Yallop rejects the earlier claims that lacemaking had been introduced to the area by Flemish refugees fleeing persecution in Europe and his research and evidence is quite compelling. He believes that new enterprises often emerged in areas that had the necessary skills that could be adapted and where materials were accessible.[48]

This is similar in thought to G. F. R. Spenceley, in his paper on The Origins of the English Pillow Lace Industry. Spenceley suggests that the impetus for the development of rural industries tended to come from within the rural community itself, as it searched for ways to supplement the meagre returns from agriculture. He goes on to say that *"the common feature among all rural industrial workers, no matter what the period of time or region in which they were employed, was poverty".*[49] A large swathe of the population of both Eye and the neighbouring villages was dependent upon agriculture and continued to be so right through to the 19th century. The area had a workforce of women and children available to work from home; the town was also well positioned on a north south route between Ipswich and Norwich through Diss; and an east west route between Lowestoft and Yarmouth to Bury St. Edmunds. Equipment was minimal and could either be made locally or in the case of thread, sourced without too much difficulty. Those with the necessary knowledge and skills could initially, be brought in to teach the local workforce and this might well explain the Flemish influence.

Levey writes that *"chance references"* during the 17th century attest *"to the widespread establishment of lace-making: in England [and that] such references occur across the country from East Anglia to Wiltshire"*,[50] adding that many of these domestic laces were often listed anonymously in household accounts, with little detail other than their quantity and that they were *"bought of a pedlar"* or from a local mercer, and used for edging a child's garment or some other household item.[51]

Penderel Moody poses the question as to why lacemakers tended to be found in villages and small country towns, and like Spenceley she concludes that it was because the country offered fewer employment opportunities and so any opportunity would be welcome. She summarises lacemaking as suitable employment for young girls and the country wife, who can fit the *"home work"* around her other duties and *"splendid work for a cripple girl, or one too delicate for service"* and allows *"the old people [to] keep their work going, often up to the very last."*[52] That Elizabeth Grimstoune was the sole lacemaker recorded in receipt of relief at the time, seems to support the theory that lacemaking was either a means of supporting an individual or a supplement to a household's income. Levey further describes the English lace industry as *"a cottage industry dependent on the labour of women and children"* and that it was often *"associated with poor relief".*[53]

It is therefore, quite reasonable to conjecture that with the rising popularity and demand for lace across the country, some entrepreneur of the day saw an opportunity to develop a new industry and the local community grasped at the chance to supplement their incomes. In lieu of more substantive evidence, this is perhaps the best explanation for how and why the industry came to be centred around the town.

Two other places in the county are also mentioned as having some association with lacemaking. The earliest comes from Blome's Britannia of 1673, where he recorded that in Needham [Market] *"the work of the poorer sort of women is spinning of wool for Clothiers, and making Bone-lace"*.[54] This is the source used by Dymond and Northeast for their map depicting industries in 17th and 18th century Suffolk.[55]

Later books such as Cox's Magna Britannia and The New General English Dictionary make no mention of lacemaking at Needham, though the simple explanation would be that the trade had ceased sometime before their publication. However, it is interesting to note that Needham lies a little to the north of Ipswich, close to where the road divides for either Bury St. Edmunds or Diss.

Glemsford is the village that T. L. Huetson mentions in his book Lace and Bobbins, it lies close to Sudbury not too far from the border with Essex. Huetson writes that he had been unable to *"associate lacemaking ......with any particular area"* but that it was *"made at one time in the Glemsford district"*.[56] I have found no further mention of lacemaking in the area which is more usually associated with silk weaving, nor have I been able to determine the source of Huetson's information.

The V&A Collection of Suffolk Lace

ESTABLISHING PROVENANCE

A visit to the V&A was arranged, to view the Suffolk lace held in the Museum's reserve collection and to see any records that might finally establish the collection's provenance. Eye's lacemaking past was in no doubt and I had a clearer picture regarding the type of lace that was made during the 19th century, but I had still only seen the piece made by the late Mary Collins and Plate LXXXVII in Palliser.

It was imperative to know just where this collection of lace had originated and the wait, while the Central Inventory accession book was being located, was a touch nerve racking. Once found, the page's contents made an exciting read, they recorded quite clearly how in 1875, the V&A had purchased *"forty-three specimens of Suffolk [lace] made edging of various patterns; bone pillow lace,"* for the sum of £10. 5s. 0d. from Revd. W. H. Sewell of Yaxley Vicarage, Eye, Suffolk. A further *"seventeen small specimens of Suffolk [lace] made edging of various patterns; bone pillow lace"* were given by Revd. W. H. Sewell to the V&A at a later date that year.

A revised printed note on the page read, *"The patterns in most of these specimens are derived from simple Mechlin, Lille, and Valenciennes patterns. The make of the lace resembles that of Buckinghamshire laces, and that of Norman laces of present time. The entire collection displays varied combinations of six ways of plaiting and twisting threads."* The margin was dated 1881 and signed Mr. A. S. Cole and was clearly the source for the quote in Palliser's 4th Edition of *A History of Lace*.[57]

It also explained why the earlier editions of her book made no mention of Suffolk lace, for the third edition was printed in 1875. On 4th April 1887 a further note was added, signed by C.W. Derby, it recorded that *"one small piece, no31 of the series"* had been *"lost in Mr Andrew's room when the pieces were being mounted."*

The provenance couldn't have been clearer, not only had the collection originated from Suffolk, but it had done so through the hands of the local vicar, some thirty two years before the Countess had begun her patronage of the Malmesbury lacemakers.

THE LACE

Seeing the samples for the first time was another exciting moment. It is not a large collection, Revd. Sewell sold/donated a total of sixty pieces including those depicted in plate LXXXVII of Palliser. All the pieces in the collection are Point Ground lace, and worked as continuous pieces rather than individual motifs which are then joined. The Central Inventory detailed two separate acquisition entries, the first comprises

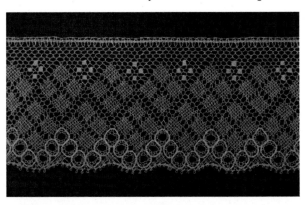

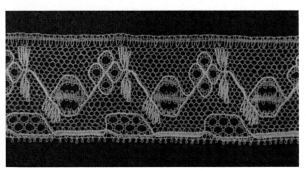

the group of pieces prefixed 1249-1875 the samples being numbered 1 to 43, the second are those prefixed 1250-1875 and numbered 1-17.

The collection comprises edgings (one straight edge for attaching to fabric) and four insertions (two straight edges for stitching to fabric) with patterns that are predominantly geometric in style, often with closely recurring repeats. Penderel Moody writes that *"'Baby' lace was the name given to edgings of less importance and value"*,[58] but it is also perhaps, a suitable description for edgings that may well have adorned many a baby's bonnet and christening gown, or in fact any garment that required the enhancement of a narrow edging.

Fig.9 Suffolk lace patterns redrawn and worked by the author

1249-1875.8D1 (above)
1249-1875.4 (below)

Of the two groups, the first is by far the larger and it was for these samples that Revd. Sewell received remuneration. Although numbered 1-43, there are in fact 44 samples, for there are two number eights differentiated as 8 and 8D1. Of this group only two pieces, those numbered 18 and 20, are of the same design. Most of the pieces in this group were of reasonable length, and were probably longer when they originally arrived at the museum. Subsequently they have been divided up and I understand that there are now around a 149 individual pieces.

The second group were given by Revd. Sewell later that same year, they were on the whole just small snippets, often only a pattern repeat or two in length. Again, although numbered 1-17 there are only 16 samples. There are no pieces numbered 11 or 13, but two samples are numbered 10.1 and 10.2. Of these sixteen pieces, 10 were of different designs to those of the first group, the remaining 6 were of designs ostensibly the same as those in the first group. Perhaps Revd. Sewell came across these oddments after having made the initial sale to the V&A, and donated them because they were just fragments.

A further and final piece, numbered 138-1883 was given to the museum in 1883, this particular piece was of the design known as "The Grecian".

In the museum's textile study room 100, a display of Suffolk lace was to be found in frame Q67.

What the Postcard Revealed

Both Bessie Copping and Margaret Cooper had identified the lacemaker in the postcard as Mary Collins of Yaxley, and this supported one of the pencilled notations on the back of my copy which read *"Miss Collins lived at Yaxley"*. The style of the postcard and her clothing dated it to the early 1900's, while the cottage setting had the appearance of a more rural location.

The lace pillow appears to be almost rectangular in shape with a slightly domed top and curving at the edges, rather like a flattened bolster pillow. It is supported on a stand called a pillow horse and is similar to many of those used in the other English lacemaking areas, with its bow shaped front and three supporting legs.

However, it is the bobbins that make this particular postcard so interesting, for unlike the more familiar East Midlands bobbins with their pretty spangles (a ring of beads), these bobbins have bulbous ends, reminiscent of those from the Low Countries.

The wooden bobbin winder standing on a small table to her left, has an open wheel made and moulded from a single length of thin wood. Only three of the central spokes are visible but their angle suggests a total of five. A wooden cross with tall pegs is attached at the back of the winder and a partial skein of thread remains wound around the pegs. The wheel would be connected to a bobbin holder by a tape or cord and when the wheel is turned, the cross would rotate on a spindle so that as the thread wound onto the bobbin, it would unwind from the skein. This all sits on top of a base which appears to have a drawer with a small central knob which is just visible at the end. It would be used to store spare bobbins and sundry odds and ends. It is very much a functional winder rather than one that has had craftsmanship lavished upon it.

Unfortunately, it's not possible to determine from the postcard the actual pattern being worked, but it is an edging rather than an insertion, because the footside (a straight edge used for attaching lace to fabric) is on the right and gentle headside curves are just visible on what would be the decorative left hand edge of the lace. It is also not one of the narrower patterns, such as the edging given to Bessie Copping, for it requires a few more bobbins and appears to be approximately two inches (5cms) wide. A reasonable length of lace has been worked, because it trails over the back of the pillow, where it is gathered into a fabric pocket hanging at the end, its purpose being to keep the lace clean. I suspect the lace has been extended like this for the benefit of the photograph.

A SUFFOLK LACE MAKER
AGED 90 YEARS
WITH ANTIQUE BOBBIN WINDER

A caption on the front of the postcard *"Sold in aid of the Universities' Mission to Central Africa"* made it clear that it was being sold for charitable works. Founded by the Universities of Oxford and Cambridge following David Livingstone's return from Africa in 1857, its purpose was to send a mission to Africa. Parish records do show that Yaxley Church held a number of fund raising events for this mission, and a postcard depicting one of Yaxley's oldest residents and most likely its last lacemaker of the period, was probably regarded as an innovative way of raising money for this cause.

*Fig.10
Mary Collins of,
Yaxley*

The reverse of the postcard gave no clues as to the identity of who had originally produced it, but this would tend to indicate that both the photography and the printing had been undertaken by someone locally. Perhaps they had even suggested the idea at a parish meeting?

A second notation in biro read *"Donated 13 June 1979, Mr Cracknell, 36 Barn Rise, Wembley Pk. Middlesex"*. To what cause it was being donated was unclear.

Who was Miss Mary Collins?

Census and parish records reveal a snapshot of Mary's life. Born at Monk Soham, just a few miles from Eye, in 1817, Mary was the eldest child of Henry and Harriett Collins née Stone. The entry for her baptism on 4 January 1818 at the parish church records her father's occupation as a blacksmith. They moved just a few miles to the village of Southolt, where her father continued working as a blacksmith.

It was in Southolt that the births of her brothers and sisters were recorded; Henry (1820); Matilda (1823) who only survived a few months; another daughter also named Matilda (1826); Sarah Anne (1829); William (1832) and finally Esther (1837) and then in January 1840 the death of her mother who was just 41 years old.

Mary, by now a young woman of 22 and the eldest daughter, would have been expected to take over the running of the household. Like many daughters of her day she would have grown up assisting her mother with the daily routine of chores, and looking after her younger siblings. She may also have helped supplement the family income with her lacemaking. By 1842 the family had moved to Eye.

The next glimpse into Mary's life is through the census records of 1851; now aged 34, she was living at Abbey Farm, once part of the former Priory, just along the Stradbroke Road on the outskirts of Eye. Here she worked for Walter Craske as a dairymaid. Meanwhile, her sister Sarah Anne was working as a housemaid at The Rectory in Yaxley for the newly inducted and soon to be married Revd. Edward Cobbold. Also resident is the late incumbent's widow Ann Sewell and young son William Henry.

Fig.11
The Street,
Yaxley

Ten years on, in 1861, Mary is also to be found living at the Vicarage in Yaxley, employed as a nurse to the children of Revd. Cobbold and his wife Matilda. Their first child was born in 1853 so it would be reasonable to suppose, that Mary's employment with the family began at this time and perhaps her sister put in a good word for her. With a further six children arriving in due course, Mary was going to be kept fully occupied. Sarah Anne is just a cottage or two away working as a housemaid for Mrs Elizabeth Pretty, grandmother of Revd. Sewell.

By 1871, the Cobbold family had moved to Folkstone in Kent, but with the children no longer in need of a nurse Mary's role within the family had changed to that of cook. Her sister, Sarah, on the other hand is again working at the Rectory in Yaxley; her position is now housekeeper for the new vicar, Revd. William Henry Sewell.

1881 and Sarah, now 51, is still working at the Vicarage for Revd. Sewell. Her sister Mary, who is 64, has retired from her employment with the Cobbold family and returned to Suffolk. At the time of the census she was boarding with James and Clara Bush in Yaxley. She is listed as an "annuitant," was this a pension agreed by Revd. Cobbold for her years of faithful service perhaps?

In the two subsequent censuses of 1891 and 1901 Mary is still living in Yaxley, but she now has her own cottage in The Street and living by her "own means". Sarah is still just a cottage or two away. Dating from the 1600's, this cottage is the setting for the two photographs depicting Mary sitting before her lace pillow; she remained here until her death in 1909 aged 92 years.

Although the census records do not show Mary employed as a lacemaker, we can be sure that she learnt her skills from an early age, and it is not unreasonable to assume that she attended a local Dame School. Usually run by elderly women in their own homes, these schools would often provide craft instruction, such as lacemaking and part of the day might be spent learning the 3 R's. However, there was no training or regulation so the quality and standard varied considerably.

Fig.12
Mary Collins seated at her lace pillow outside the cottage at Yaxley. Mary is perhaps a little younger in this photograph, her face is a little fuller, but she does appear to be wearing the same hat, her Sunday best?

The distinctive bobbins are wound with plenty of thread.

The strip of lace worked by Mary and subsequently given to Bessie Copping (pictured below) is a simple Point Ground edging, very similar to one of the samples in the V&A collection (1250-1875.7). It is also reminiscent of a pattern known to lacemakers as "Sheep's Head" with the thicker gimp thread outlining small blocks of honeycomb stitch. At ½" or 1.25cms wide it requires just 14 pairs of bobbins.

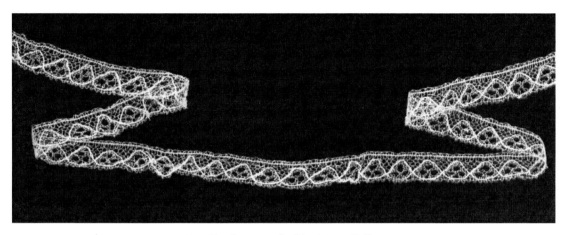

Fig.13   Lace worked by Mary Collins
Photograph by Gerry Pitcher, courtesy of Geoff Caulton

Suffolk Bobbin Finds

PEST HOUSE OR POCKY HOUSE, EYE

Tucked away on the outskirts of the town stands a two storey timber framed building dating from the early 18th century. During renovation work on the property in the late 1970's, four wooden bobbins were found when a ground floor ceiling was demolished, a further bobbin was discovered later, in the rubble. They still had thread wound on and each measured about 3½" (9cms) in length and one in particular showed signs of having been gnawed, probably by either rats or mice.

It is believed that the building was once used as an isolation house for those suffering with an infectious disease, hence its name, but by 1841 it had become home to four families. The family of Robert and Mary Woods was of particular interest for they lived in one of the large rooms for at least ten years and two daughters, Elizabeth and Louisa, worked as lacemakers. Elizabeth married Joseph Keeley, whose mother and aunt were lacemakers and their daughter Elizabeth also became a lacemaker. Louisa later returned to live with her parents at the cottage after her first husband died, as did Robert and Mary's grandchildren, so it is perhaps not so surprising that lace bobbins came to be found.

DOVE HOUSE, LAMBSETH STREET, EYE

A listed building, this property, left foreground Fig.14 was originally two cottages. The left half having a single window and door was built c.1540 while the right half has three windows and a differently pitched roof and dates from the early 17th century.

Two bobbins were found to the left of the wide main door when the ground floor ceiling of the tea room was demolished. Both the bobbins, one measuring a little over 3½" (9cms) long, the other barely 3" (8cms), had been well chewed during their time hidden beneath the floorboards of the first floor.

In 1841, lacemaker Sophia Sivill was living at one of the cottages shown in the photograph.

By 1851 William Everson and his family had also moved into one of the cottages. His daughter Mary Ann was also a lacemaker.

Fig.14 Lambseth Street, Eye

SHINGLE HOUSE, CHURCH STREET, EYE

In 1982, two more bobbins along with three shoes, a cotton spool, a two pronged fork, a broken mug and shards of Delft pottery, were discovered behind the chimney breast of Shingle House, which dates from the 16th century.

The bobbins (Fig.15), were again just like the other finds and even had thread still intact. One other item of great interest amongst this small haul was an old parchment pricking. This collection of items was donated to Ipswich Museum in 1982/83, but prior to their donation Geoff Caulton was able to examine both the bobbins and pricking. Fortunately he also made a copy of the pricking, for it has since gone missing. The pricking appears to be of a very simple Torchon type pattern similar to one known as "Four Penny Spot", with a fan headside and diamonds forming the main design.

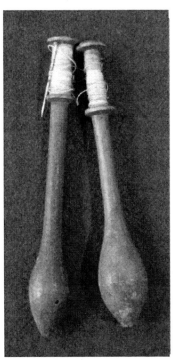

Fig.15 Photograph by author, courtesy of Colchester & Ipswich Museum Service

MAYNARDS CHEMIST, BROAD STREET, EYE

The shop standing on the corner of Church Street and Broad Street, dating back to c.1460. has undergone various extensions and remodelling, much of which was

Fig.16 Maynard's Chemist

undertaken during the 17th and 18th centuries. It has been used primarily as a chemists shop since at least the mid 1860's when it was taken over by William S. Nurse soon after he returned to Eye with his family from America.

Joan Maynard showed me the attic room, formerly used for servants quarters, where the single bobbin was discovered when insulation was being installed.

It has been said that none of these bobbins *"could have accidentally fallen where they lay"* but that they had been *"placed there possibly for superstitious reasons"*.[59] This is not a theory that I personally agree with. Having worked with bobbins of this type I have on occasions accidentally dropped one and so seen first hand how the bulbous end allows them to roll around on an uncarpeted floor. The attic room still has its old wide floor boards with a number of "old" worn gaps, that would easily allow a rolling bobbin to slip through, and so remain hidden for many years. I believe this to be a more likely explanation for bobbins being found where they are.

*Fig. 17 Lowgate Street, Eye, a number of the cottages
depicted were once homes to the towns lacemakers*

THE BULL, YAXLEY

As recounted previously, bobbins were discovered at the The Bull, by Roy and Margaret Buttle. The five bobbins, as can be seen in Fig. 18 are like all the others. The Bull is a former coaching inn, situated beside the A140 Ipswich to Norwich road. Former landlords went by the surnames of Jeffries, Bullingham, Nunn, all names that occur amongst the lacemakers, coincidence maybe. One particularly notable landlord recorded in the census of 1901 was Arthur Cracknell and his wife Mary Jane - they turned out to be the parents of the late Edward Cracknell of Barn Rise, Wembley, who donated the postcard of Mary Collins to the unknown cause, which I later came to acquire.

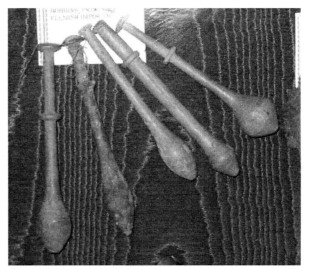

Fig.18 Bobbins on display at "The Bull" Yaxley

MILLINER'S PRESS COTTAGE, MELLIS ROAD, YAXLEY

A single bobbin was found under the stairs by Bob Cotton. The under stair space which had a dry earth floor, had until then been completely sealed off. Nothing more is known.

OTHER LOCAL FINDS

Various snippets of information have been passed on to me, often through "a friend of a friend" which I have as yet been unable to corroborate, but I understand that over the years bobbins have been found at the following properties -:

7 Lowgate Street, Eye	2 bobbins & other items
2 Church Street, Eye	1 or 2 bobbins
Langton Green, Eye	1 bobbin
Cottage, Thorndon	2 bobbins under a window sill
Old Thatch, Goldbrook, Hoxne	1 bobbin in ceiling space
Cottage, Debenham	1 bobbin behind the fireplace

Any further information about these bobbins or indeed any other lace related item from the area would be most welcome and may be sent to me at the contact address given elsewhere in the book.

Suffolk Bobbins

The bobbins discovered around Eye, during the 1980's all show a remarkable similarity to bobbins used by the lacemakers of the Low Countries, with their distinctive single head and bulbous end. It does seem to suggest a Flemish connection with the Suffolk industry at some time in its past. Could it be that Flemish lacemakers were brought over to teach their skills to the local workforce and brought their bobbins with them?

My own thoughts lead me to believe that these particular bobbins were probably made by local craftsmen, who had continued making them in the style that had been adopted and passed down through the generations. There were certainly local men with both the skills and the means for turning such bobbins. That neither the censuses nor the trade directories identify anyone specifically as a "bobbin maker", leads me to believe that they were being made as a side line to their regular work, and would perhaps explain why the bobbins remained quite plain. Variations in the shape of the head and bulbous end also suggests that they were turned by different makers.

Dating them is also difficult, though from their appearance and condition, it would not be unreasonable to believe that they had been made sometime in the 19th century, but it is quite feasible for them to be older. We know that bobbins of this type were certainly being made in the late 16th and early 17th centuries, because of various discoveries such as that made in the 1960's on a shipwreck off Australia's western coast. Amongst the haul was a small fragment of lace and three wooden lace bobbins, two of which were fully intact. These bobbins underwent cleaning and conservation treatment and were found to be similar in style to those depicted in paintings by Dutch artists Casper Netscher *The Lace-Maker* (1662) and Stephen van Duyven *Sleeping Lace-Maker* (1667), and to bobbins dating from about 1580 to 1634, excavated from the site of St Luciënklooster orphanage in Amsterdam. The ship was the Batavia, owned by the Dutch East India Company. She had embarked on her maiden voyage to Batavia (modern Jakarta), but was wrecked on Morning Reef on 4 June 1629.[60] Two of the Batavia bobbins, one incomplete, are very like those found in Suffolk (see overleaf).

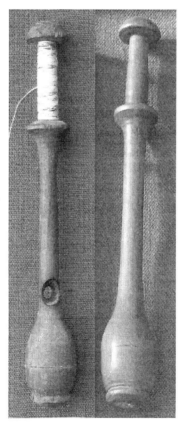

Fig. 19
Note the similarity between the bobbin found at Yaxley on the left and the Flemish bobbin right

photograph (right)
Brian Lemin

One aspect that does intrigue me is that unlike the lace bobbins of the East Midlands, which evolved from quite plain bobbins to those with spangles, the Suffolk bobbins have remained unchanged. Perhaps it serves to demonstrate a lack of contact between the lace industry of Suffolk and those located elsewhere in England?

Fig.20 Suffolk bobbins discovered in properties in and around Eye
Photograph Gerry Pitcher, courtesy of Geoff Caulton

Fig.21 Bobbins from the shipwreck Batavia, note the similarity
of the lower bobbin to those of Suffolk

Photograph courtesy of Western Australian Museum

The Misses Wright and their Collection

The sisters, Florence, Ada and Lily, were the daughters of James Wright and Eliza Brown. They were all born in Eye, Florence in 1882, Ada in 1885 and Lily the youngest, a year later. Their father was originally from Salhouse in Norfolk, but had moved to the town by the mid 1870's. A master baker, he initially set up business in Cross Street, but by 1891 the family had moved to premises in Broad Street.

Fig.22 James Wright's shop on Broad Street is the first building on the left
his name is just visible above the shop front

Their mother, however, was very much a local girl, in fact her aunt and uncle, James and Martha Brown, are recorded living in one of the large rooms at the town's Pest House, along with the Woods family in the 1851 census. Eliza grew up just a stones throw away from them in Back Lane, while a couple of doors away lived Mary Collins' brother with his family. It was very much a small market town community where everyone knew each other.

After the death of their father in 1928, the business was taken over by their brother Harry, but by 1937, the business in Broad Street had again changed its name to Misses F.A. & L. Wright, reflecting the names of the three sisters. They are fondly remembered for wearing plenty of face powder and rouge and locals also recall, how their cat would sit amongst the buns and sweets! Florence died in 1968 her sister Lily two years later.

Who actually taught the sisters to make lace is not known, but it is thought that they learnt before the First World War. It may even be that it was their mother who taught them, for it is quite possible that she learnt to make lace as a child.

It was apparently the Executor for the late Misses Wright, who passed a collection of their belongings into the custody of Eye Town Council. In June 1977, Mr Triggs the Town Clerk, received a letter from Col. John Busby, informing him that he and his wife had now inspected the box of lace making material in the Council Chambers, and suggested that apart from the bobbin winder which could be repaired, *"the other items [were] of little value"* and should be offered *"to Ipswich Museum for inclusion in their collections or disposal"*.

The Council, having passed the collection into the care of Ipswich Museum received a letter from curator Patricia Butler, in which she recounted how *"one of the two lace winders fell to bits as soon as we looked at it and the wood-worm could be seen poking out of the embroidery frame"*. She added that the other lace-winding machine and bobbins were all *"being treated"*. A subsequent letter to Mr. Triggs, informed him of the museums reference number and listed the collection as comprising *"a quantity of common lace bobbins, wooden lace-winding machine, short lengths of coarse, pillow-made lace, a needle book with pin-cushion"* and dates the collection as being *"early 20th century"*.[61]

Having arranged a visit to Ipswich Museum to view the collection, I was delighted to find around 200 bobbins that were again just like the other finds, though a few showed some rather fancy turning (see page 36). They were an absolute joy to handle, and were generally in excellent condition, perhaps a half dozen with damaged heads. A good number had suffered various small chips and dents, but these had been gradually worn smooth through use in a lacemakers hands. Judging from the slight differences in colour, a number of woods had been used to make them, but each had developed a lovely patina which comes with age and use.

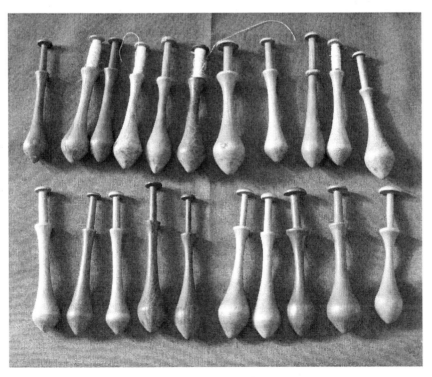

Fig. 23 These bobbins were grouped together because of their similarity to bobbins found at The Bull, Yaxley (Fig.18)

Photograph by author, courtesy of Colchester & Ipswich Museum Service

Page 35 shows two groups of bobbins still attached to short lengths of lace, which are also part of the Misses Wright Collection. One piece is a simple Bedfordshire pattern, while the other is Torchon lace. It is quite likely that both pieces were worked by one or other of the sisters, possibly in the 1960's. Who removed the lace and bobbins from their lace pillows is not known, but one assumes it was prior to the collection being handed over to the Town Council. It would also seem that their pillows, probably with the prickings still pinned to them, were disposed of which is a great shame.

Having spent time handling the bobbins and many hours looking at various photographs of them, it is again my opinion, that they are not 20th century bobbins, but that they also, like the others, date from the 19th century at least. It is also my belief that they, along with the winders and other items such as pillows, now lost to us, were passed down to the sisters through the maternal side of the family. We are very fortunate that someone recognised the potential importance of what remains of this collection and passed it into the care of Eye Town Council, for had they not done so it is doubtful that this wonderful collection of bobbins would have survived.

At the time of writing it has not as yet been possible to study the remaining bobbin winder, as both Ipswich Museum and Christchurch Mansion are undergoing roof repairs and the reserve collections are inaccessible to researchers.

Revd. W. H. Sewell, MA. Vicar of Yaxley

Through my research into Mary Collins, I had begun to learn more about Revd. Sewell. Connections between them kept cropping up and I hoped that gradually it might help me to understand why he sold the lace to the V&A.

William Henry Sewell, was the eldest son of Henry and Ann. Like both his parents, he was born in Eye, the town having been home to both families for several generations. According to Pigot's Directory of 1839 his father and maternal grandmother, Elizabeth Pretty were patrons of a school in Lambseth Street, their pupils coming from the town's wealthier families.

Henry Sewell had been preparing to enter the ministry for some years, and this led to the family moving to Yaxley when he became the curate in 1846. Unusually, he also held the advowson for the parish which ensured the living for his son in the future.[62] William went on to study and graduate from Trinity College, Cambridge, in 1858 and having served as curate at Halstead, Essex, he returned to Yaxley in 1861 to take up the incumbency.

Fig.24 Image of Revd. Sewell in a stained glass window at Yaxley Church

He recorded various reminiscences which spanned not only the years of his father's curacy, but those of his own time as Vicar of Yaxley. In his Memoranda Book he recorded for example, that labourers maintained the tradition of sitting on the north nave while their wives sat in the south, writing *"why should we not all keep to the good old ways?"*. The restoration of the church was something that he was clearly quite passionate about, documenting that it *"was neither wind nor water-tight"* and continues to detail the many obstacles he faced, in persuading the various authorities to undertake the necessary repairs.[63]

Sarah Ann, sister to Mary Collins, kept house for him throughout his years in Yaxley. Having known her since a boy, it is none too surprising that he should have made provision for her upon his death, ensuring that Sarah might remain living at Rose Cottage, purchased by him in 1872, for *"the remainder of her life"*.[64]

But what of the lace? I think William collected and purchased it from the last few elderly lacemakers in the area, the younger ones having discarded their pillows for the flax works. He clearly cared about both local tradition and preserving the work of what had once been a significant and flourishing local industry and perchance saw the V&A as a suitable custodian for it. There can be little doubt that this collection is the industry's remnant, and as such, may not represent the best of Suffolk's lace, but I do believe that more of the area's 'baby lace' lies unknown in collections elsewhere. However, because of the philanthropy of William Sewell, we at least have some examples of the work by the lacemakers of this forgotten industry.

Revd. William Henry Sewell died suddenly on 14th November 1896, he was buried at Yaxley.

Fig. 25 A section of the stained glass window erected in memory or Revd. W. H. Sewell.

30

John Chauntler - Lace Dealer

Having carried out fairly extensive searches of the Suffolk censuses, it seemed to me that I was missing someone ...... a lace dealer. Even allowing for the fact that the industry was beginning to wane by the mid 19th century, there were still over two hundred lacemakers working, so somebody had to be selling the lace for them. There was of course the article in the Ipswich Journal of 1821, previously mentioned, regarding the pedlars *"supposedly from Eye"* who had been travelling *"about the parishes of Walton and Kirton selling British Lace"*,[65] and Penderel Moody also writes that lace was often *"bought by pedlars who carried it far afield in their baskets [to sell]"*.[66] I wasn't entirely convinced that pedlars were the sole solution to selling the quantities of lace that would have been produced, so where was the lace dealer?

I little expected to find an answer, to this question while trawling through the parish records for St. Matthew's, Ipswich, but that is exactly how I found the entry made on 5th September 1846 for the marriage of *"Lace Dealer"* John Chauntler to Elizabeth Fuller Backhouse.

Elizabeth was the 23 year old daughter of Benjamin and Mary Ann Backhouse née Prentice. Benjamin had begun his working life as a builder and went on to become both an architect and building surveyor. Major projects that he was involved with, include the Corn Exchange and Thingoe Union House at Bury St Edmunds and in Ipswich, the East Suffolk Hospital, Anglesea Road, designed by William Ribbans.

Fig.26 Family of Elizabeth Backhouse once lived at this Terrace along the Norwich Road

Further research into the family showed that they had once lived along Ipswich's Norwich Road. Curiosity led me to dig a little deeper, for the address rang a few bells, and sure enough, it transpired that it was indeed the very house where I had once rented a second floor flat over thirty years earlier!

At the time of John Chauntler's marriage to Elizabeth, he was living at 20 Friday Street, Cheapside, London. His father, also named John, was recorded as a *"Gentleman"*, which inferred that his son born in 1809, had grown up in relative prosperity in the Staplehurst /Hawkhurst area of Kent.

So how did a London Lace Dealer meet and come to marry a young woman from Ipswich? Business, seems to be the most likely answer, for he does not appear to have had any other connection with Suffolk. He is first recorded in 1841 working in London as a linen draper and residing at Gracechurch Street, but by 1843/44 the Trade Directories list him as a *"laceman"*, trading in his own right from 51 St Paul's Churchyard. Whether he purchased and took over an existing business, is unclear, but this is perhaps the most likely time for his travels to Suffolk to have begun, for he would have been establishing the business and seeking to strengthen any connections that he may have bought into. Meanwhile, the census shows Elizabeth apparently working at a draper's shop in Woodbridge. Is this how their acquaintance began?

As a lace dealer Chauntler would have supplied the lacemakers with the necessary patterns and thread. Being based in London, Suffolk was probably not his only source and this may well have brought about patterns travelling from one area to another. However, the business was clearly flourishing, for by 1851, John and Elizabeth were now residing with two daughters at 5 Lowndes Terrace, Knightsbridge. John was also employing six assistants, one of whom happened to be Elizabeth's younger sister, Rebecca. Lowndes Terrace seems to have been a highly industrious area, the censuses record almost every property occupied with drapers, stay makers and silk mercers, and all with numerous assistants and various employees. It was not just the Chauntler's home that was a hive of industry, for John was still trading from his warehouse at St. Paul's Churchyard, dealing in lace, millinery and baby linen. By 1871, the Chauntler's had moved premises, just a few yards along Lowndes Terrace to number 12, where they remained until John finally retired. Neither of his sons took up the business and the final directory entry for it appears in the 1873/74 edition. Through the directories I began to build up a picture of the neighbourhood, and it became evident that from around 1866, the properties comprising Lowndes Terrace were gradually being bought up by a rapidly growing linen drapery business, and number 12 was one of their final purchases - the business was Harvey Nicholls.

Fig.27 Harvey Nicholls, Kensington.

John and Elizabeth moved to the leafy suburb of Streatham, where John died in 1885. He made generous provision in his will for his wife, two sons and seven daughters, leaving them an estate valued at £11,673, which in today's money equates to around £640,000.

The source of John's lace is not known for certain, and speculation regarding his involvement with the Suffolk industry in its latter years is not unreasonable, for the 'baby lace' from Eye was clearly suited to his trade. Is it coincidence that Revd. Sewell sold the remnants of the Suffolk industry to the V&A just months after Chauntler's retirement? I think perhaps not.

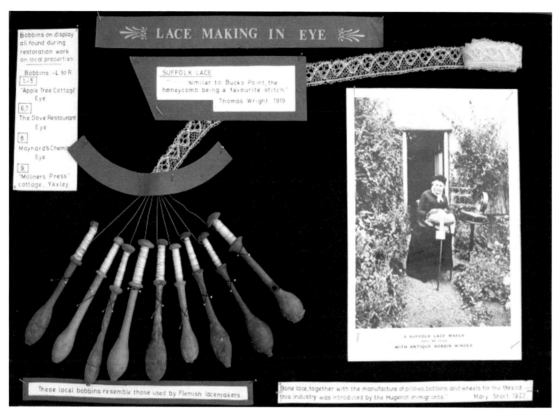

Lace bobbins together with a postcard of Mary Collins and the piece of lace made by her, mounted for the 'Eye in the Past' Exhibition held at the parish church in 1981.

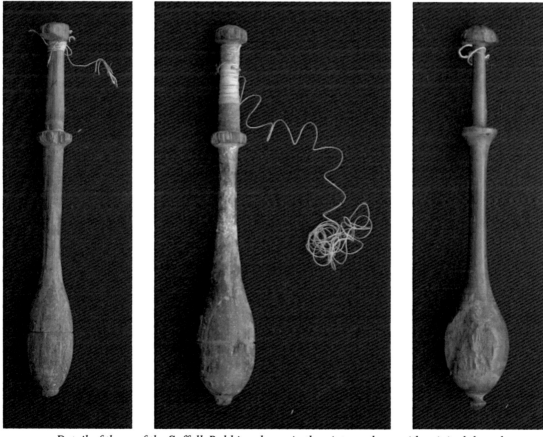

Detail of three of the Suffolk Bobbins shown in the picture above with original thread still attached, the wear and damage to them is clearly visible.

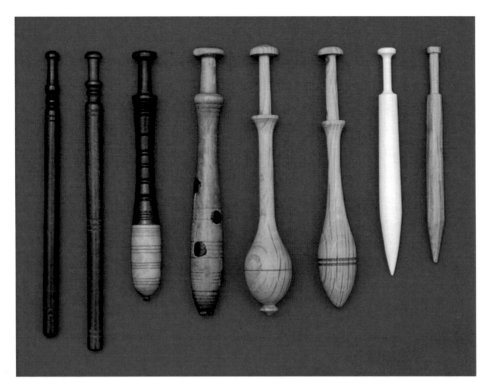

A selection of English regional bobbins (left to right)
Malmesbury; Bucks Thumpers; Suffolk (replicas), Downton, and below

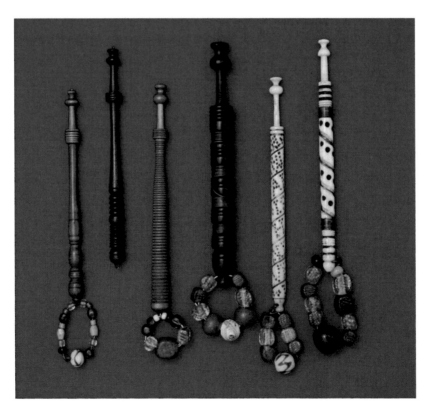

East Midlands. Note that the spangles of the three bobbins on the right are attached by a wire passing through a hole drilled at the bottom, while those on the left have their spangles attached by means of a staple which is clearly visible on the bobbin missing its spangle.

34

*Two bundles of tangled bobbins still attached to lengths of lace
from the Misses Wright Collection*

Photographs by author, courtesy of Colchester & Ipswich Museum Service

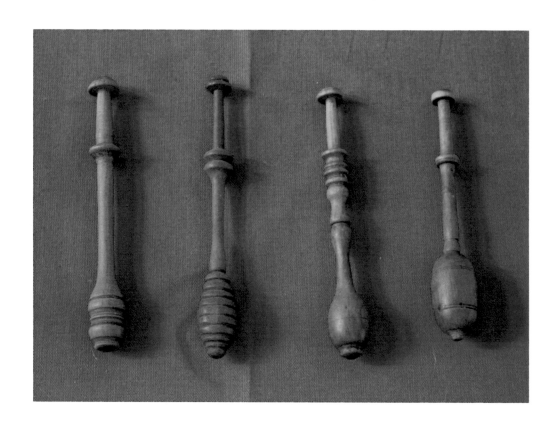

A further selection of bobbins from the Misses Wright Collection.
Those above have been turned with rather more decoration than usual,
all the bobbins have a lovely patina.

Photographs by author, courtesy of Colchester & Ipswich Museum Service

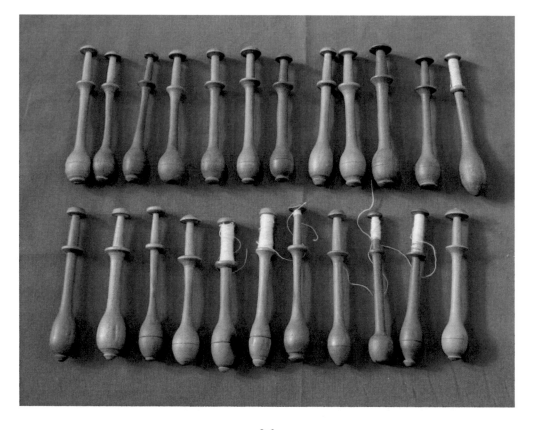

2. THE LACEMAKERS OF EYE

As I trawled through census and parish records seeking to identify the lacemakers, certain names kept recurring and tangled webs of kinship began to emerge. Today we take travel so much for granted, but then, distance tended to restrict courtship to within a circle of neighbouring villages. Families would thus inter-marry both over and across successive generations, and it is not uncommon to discover family groups of the same surname within a small area being either closely or distantly related. Like the lace they made, the web of these relationships became more complex the further back one looked.

The following list details all the women and girls in the area who have to date been identified as a lacemaker between 1837 and 1861. Unsurprisingly, the spelling of names often varied between documents and was also dependent upon the interpretation of the person writing it down. In some instances I suspect that a broad Suffolk dialect may well have misled the writer into some of the more interesting examples that I came across. So for the purpose of this list I have used the variant which appeared most consistently within the records. Where a subsequent marriage has been identified this additional surname has been listed in sequence.

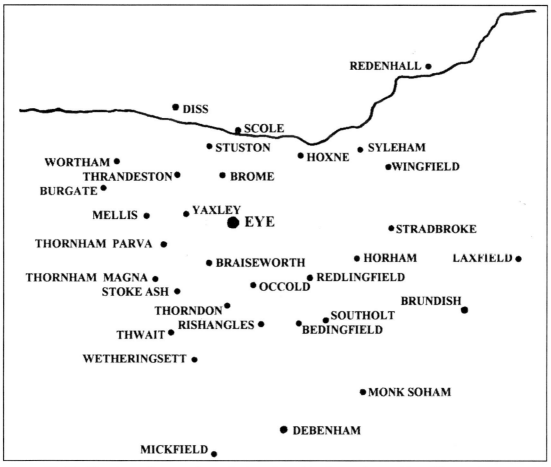

Fig.28 The above diagram shows the location of the known lacemaking villages, they are predominantly south of the Norfolk border and within a five mile radius of Eye.

Name	Surname - Maiden & Married		Year & Place of Birth	
Abigail	Emes	Rampling	1820	Eye
Amelia	Aubin	Titlow / Woodthorpe	1820	Occold
Ann	Airy	Harvey	1816	Eye
Ann	Bennett	Neobard	1824	Eye
Ann	Betts		1807	Yaxley
Ann	Burrows		1834	Eye
Ann	Hyde	Pulfer	1806	Eye
Ann	Knights	Jackson	1841	Eye
Ann	Lawrence	Bowell	1836	Eye
Ann	Leggett		1835	Yaxley
Ann	Peck	Cason	1826	Eye
Ann	Pooley		1839	Eye
Ann	Rose	Franks	1815	Yaxley
Ann	Sherman	Tuffs	1795	Eye
Ann	Stannard	Prime / Burrows	1810	Brome
Ann	Woods	Tuffs	1821	Eye
Bertha	Bacon	Williams	1829	Eye
Caroline	Bloomfield	Cousins	1831	Eye
Caroline	Calver		1828	Eye
Caroline	Chambers	Fairweather	1822	Southolt
Caroline	Elsey	——	1821	Occold
Caroline	Howard	Bond	1821	Yaxley
Caroline	Jeffries	Howard / Bond	1824	Yaxley
Caroline	Peck		1820	Rishangles
Caroline	Salter	White	1814	Wortham
Caroline	Thorndike	——	1825	Eye
Caroline	Tufts		1836	Eye
Catherine	Threadgal	——	1790	Occold
Catherine	Wells	Laws	1828	Stradbroke
Charlotte	Barnes	Jefferies	1787	Brome
Charlotte	Dade	Chinea	1833	Eye
Charlotte	Dean		1819	Stoke Ash
Charlotte	Goold	Thorndike	1830	Thornham
Charlotte	Ward	Knapp / Chenery	1808	Brome
Clemence	Civel	Everson	1785	Occold
Clementine	Perry	Wythe	1817	Occold
Delilah	Wythe		1839	Brundish

Name	Surname - Maiden & Married		Year & Place of Birth	
Editha	Clark	Lawrence	1806	Eye
Eliza	Abbott		1827	Stoke Ash
Eliza	Bennett	Marriott	1835	Eye
Eliza	Burrows	White	1822	Eye
Eliza	Canham	Last	1811	Occold
Eliza	Keeley	Carter	1834	Eye
Eliza	Peck		1834	Eye
Eliza	Perry	Gilman	1832	Eye
Eliza	Prime	Calver	1827	Yaxley
Eliza(beth)	Beales		1820	Eye
Eliza(beth)	Blomfield		1839	Yaxley
Eliza(beth)	Kemp		1833	Thornham Magna
Eliza(beth)	Holmes	Beales	1812	Eye
Eliza(beth)	Penny		1816	SFK
Eliza(beth)	Wells	Kerridge	1831	Eye
Elizabeth		Kinnell	1789	SFK
Elizabeth	Blumfield		1837	Yaxley
Elizabeth	Bond		1832	Yaxley
Elizabeth	Bond	Bloomfield	1830	Yaxley
Elizabeth	Bowell	Murdock	1773	Eye
Elizabeth	Canham		1828	Occold
Elizabeth	Cook		1835	Occold
Elizabeth	Dade	Pooley	1806	Eye
Elizabeth	Everson		1823	Occold
Elizabeth	Fulcher		1835	Occold
Elizabeth	Gardiner	Tufts	1808	Occold
Elizabeth	Garrod	Garrod	1817	Thorndon
Elizabeth	Gooderham	Everson	1838	Occold
Elizabeth	Harvey		1840	Occold
Elizabeth	Howlett	Last	1804	Stuston
Elizabeth	Kinnell	Gardiner	1816	Scole NFK
Elizabeth	Moss		1786	Occold
Elizabeth	Neobard	Hyde	1780	Eye
Elizabeth	Peck	Stockings	1832	Eye
Elizabeth	Perry		1824	Eye
Elizabeth	Taylor		1831	Yaxley
Elizabeth	Woods	Keeley	1811	Eye

Name	Surname - Maiden & Married		Year & Place of Birth	
Ellen	Cason	Thorndike	1832	Eye
Ellen	Chambers	Durrant	1825	Eye
Ellen	Ellis	Everson	1832	Bedingfield
Ellenor	Fulcher	Fulcher	1819	Occold
Emily	Aldridge	Bond	1830	Yaxley
Emily	Neobard	Bond	1824	Yaxley
Emma		Haddock	1819	Occold
Emma	Clarke	Driver	1811	Eye
Emma	Holmes		1834	Diss NFK
Emma	Leggett	——	1834	Yaxley
Emma	Ling	——	1838	Occold
Emma	Reynolds	Threadgill	1837	Occold
Emma	Torbell	Murdock	1816	Occold
Emma	Wells		1831	Eye
Ethelinda	Butcher	Williams	1838	Yaxley
Frances	Clarke	Cason	1797	Eye
Frances	Everson	——	1824	Occold
Hannah	Adams	Hunt	1814	Occold
Hannah	Bate	Chambers	1810	Eye
Hannah	Durrant	Self	1823	Debenham
Hannah	Jolly		1835	Eye
Hannah	Osborne	Nunn	1810	Thrandeston
Hannah	Stannard	Watling	1841	Thwaite
Harriet	Bird		1833	Stoke Ash
Harriet	Cooper	Bloomfield	1838	Yaxley
Harriet	Fulcher	Etheridge	1833	Syleham
Harriet	Gooderham	Cason	1790	Eye
Harriet	Gooderham	Ellis	1824	Occold
Harriet	Hawes	Canfer	1830	Yaxley
Harriet	Leftly	Bryant / Leader	1809	Wingfield
Harriet	Madget	Taylor	1821	Yaxley
Harriet	Nunn	Keeley	1787	Eye
Harriet	Taylor		1842	Yaxley
Harriett		Thenkettle	1804	Southolt
Harriett	Jeffries	Holmes	1823	Eye
Harriett	Ling		1832	Occold
Harriett	Pooley		1828	Eye

Name	Surname - Maiden & Married		Year & Place of Birth	
Isabella	Oakes		1833	Yaxley
Jane		Noller	1824	Stoke Ash
Jane		Stannard	1816	Occold
Jane	Banham	Harrison / Bloomfield	1832	Occold
Jane	Durrant		1844	Occold
Jane	Ship	Bloomfield	1840	Occold
Jemima	Marks	Fellingham	1793	Mellis
Jemima	Todd	Thorndike	1815	Eye
Jemima	Warren	Copping	1820	Thornham Magna
Lettittia	Howes	Revell	1816	Redlingfield
Lettitia	Marriott	Holmes	1789	Eye
Louisa	Chambers	Borrett	1805	Eye
Louisa	Hawes	Butcher	1818	Yaxley
Louisa	Woods	Havers / Howard	1814	Eye
Lucy	Norman	Lay	1831	Eye
Lydia	Bryant		1836	Eye
Lydia	Burrows		1834	Eye
Mahala	Pulfer	Brown	1796	Eye
Mahala	Wells		1835	Eye
Margaret	Bultitude		1837	Eye
Margaret	Rayner	Clarke	1820	Edinburgh
Maria		Atkins	1796	Eye
Maria		Welton	1805	Eye
Maria	Boston	Callick	1807	Eye
Maria	Burrows	———	1837	Eye
Maria	Canfer	Wilby	1832	Yaxley
Maria	Cason		1834	Eye
Maria	Godderham		1825	Occold
Maria	Hines	Durrant / Bond	1829	Eye
Maria	Holmes	Marriott	1835	Eye
Maria	Hunt		1837	Occold
Maria	Jefferies	Marriott	1827	Eye
Maria	Nunn	Hayward	1834	Burgate
Maria	Todd	Kerry	1817	Eye
Martha	Gooderham	Jefferies	1822	Eye
Martha	Jefferies	Leeder	1821	Eye

Name	Surname - Maiden & Married		Year & Place of Birth	
Martha	Newstead		1835	Eye
Mary		Perry	1796	Eye
Mary		Perry	1788	Eye
Mary	Aldous	Burrows	1819	Eye
Mary	Anness	Mays	1822	Thwaite
Mary	Bond		1820	Mellis
Mary	Canham		1836	Occold
Mary	Chambers	Burrows	1797	Eye
Mary	Cooke	Booty	1804	Eye
Mary	Dade		1838	Eye
Mary	Everson	Oakes	1835	Thorndon
Mary	Everson	Brewington	1809	Thorndon
Mary	Fulcher		1842	Occold
Mary	Fulcher	Everson	1829	Syleham
Mary	Green	Pooley	1800	Thornham Parva
Mary	Herbert	Kerry	1801	Eye
Mary	Kinnell	Peck	1801	Eye
Mary	Knoller	Noller	1839	Eye
Mary	Ling		1803	Eye
Mary	Neobard	Berry	1794	Yaxley
Mary (Ann)	Betts	Rockett	1794	Yaxley
Mary (Ann)	Bond	Green	1829	Eye
Mary Ann	Bond		1834	Yaxley
Mary Ann	Bryant	Turner	1833	Eye
Mary Ann	Canham	Parker	1839	Occold
Mary Ann	Ellis	Tuffs	1834	Bedingfield
Mary Ann	Everson		1816	Braiseworth
Mary Ann	Everson		1813	Occold
Mary Ann	Everson	Smith	1847	Occold
Mary Ann	Farrow	Barrett	1825	Eye
Mary Ann	Goddard		1833	Yaxley
Mary Ann	Howard		1836	Stoke Ash
Mary Ann	Knights		1835	Eye
Matilda	Brett		1825	Bedingfield
Matilda	Bryant	Chambers	1836	Eye
Matilda	Johnson	——	1803	Redenhall NFK
Miriam	Jefferies	——	1822	Eye

Name	Surname - Maiden & Married		Year & Place of Birth	
Myram	Hunt		1840	Occold
Pamela	Pollard	——	1809	Stoke Ash
Pamilla	Reade		1799	Eye
Pheby	Quinton	——	1823	Wetheringsett
Phoebe	Bultitude	Jessup	1828	Eye
Phoebe	Flatt	——	1824	Eye
Rebecca	Bultitude	Cook	1822	Eye
Rebecca	Keely	Ablett / Gooderham	1821	Occold
Rosalind	Durrant	Moore	1840	Occold
Salome	Barrett	Ablett	1823	Yaxley
Salome	Canfer	Aldridge	1835	Yaxley
Salome	Leggett	Neale	1838	Yaxley
Sapiah	Everson		1841	Occold
Sarah	Warren	Emes	1774	Eye
Sarah	Ward	Jessop	1773	Horham
Sarah	Atkins	Rayner	1814	Eye
Sarah	Bond	Cooper	1816	Yaxley
Sarah	Burridge	Gooderham	1842	Eye
Sarah	Burridge	——	1798	Eye
Sarah	Denny	——	1808	Occold
Sarah	Driver	Reynolds	1811	Thorndon
Sarah	Elvan	Sharman	1813	Stuston
Sarah	Everson	——	1798	Occold
Sarah	Lenny	——	1782	Mickfield
Sarah	Moore	Borrett	1812	Eye
Sophia	Aubin		1810	Occold
Sophia	Boston	Dykes	1819	Eye
Sophia	Bowell	Dade	1834	Eye
Sophia	Cason	——	1810	Yaxley
Sophia	Caten	Masters	1817	Occold
Sophia	Chambers	Burrows	1826	Eye
Sophia	Neobard	Bloomfield	1808	Yaxley
Sophia	Oakes	——	1806	Yaxley
Sophia	Rose	Howard	1813	Yaxley
Sophie	Sivill		1803	Eye
Susan	Durrant	Theobald	1821	SFK

Name	Surname - Maiden & Married		Year & Place of Birth	
Susan	Leggett	Bullingham	1840	Yaxley
Susan	Sharp	Grimes	1818	Occold
Susan(na)	Bond	Jefferies	1822	Mellis
Susan(na)	Lawrence	——	1788	Eye
Susan(nah)	Rumsby		1834	Occold
Susannah	Everson	Drysdale	1836	Occold

The Strays

As often happens there are always the few who don't quite fit the box!

Name	Surname—Maiden & Married		Year & Place of Birth	
Ann		Ward	c.1785?	unknown
Mary	Richerson		1824	not SFK
Mary		Durrant	1773	Tendring ESX
Susan(nah)	Durrant	Cutting	1805	Wix ESX
Elizabeth	Moore	Fildew	1809	Ipswich SFK
Mary Ann	Howard		1829	Suffolk

One such stray was found in the baptism records for Holy Trinity, Bungay. The entry dated 2 November 1814, reads "Charlotte Ward, daughter of Ann, lacemaker". To date I have discovered nothing further about them than this, nor have I found any other mention to lacemakers in Bungay, which at the time, seemed to favour the silk weaving industry.

Three others were found in the census records for Ipswich. Mary Richerson aged 17 is recorded in 1841 living at Fore Hamlet, no other members of her family are mentioned but notably her birth is recorded as "not in the county". So where did she learn to make lace?

Mother and daughter, Mary Durrant and Susan Cutting are residing at Lower Orwell Street in the census for 1851. From the information given it is ascertained that Susan's daughter, Amelia, was born in Ipswich c.1820, so they had lived in the area for at least 31 years and continued to do so for the remainder of their lives.

The final two strays, may of course be complete red herrings. Elizabeth Fildew and Mary Ann Howard are both recorded as having been born in Suffolk. Both women are also recorded as being lacemakers in Devon, Elizabeth was living in Honiton and Mary Ann at Branscombe, the two villages are well known for their lacemaking, but where did they learn to make lace - Devon or Suffolk?

As the number of lacemakers grew it could have been quite easy for them to become a mere list of names, but occasional snippets of information, usually a sorrow, would serve as a reminder. Life in rural Suffolk was often hard, Revd. Richard Cobbold in his account of Wortham, allows us a glimpse into that of lacemaker Caroline Salter, for he says of her father, William that *"this poor man was once better off in the world than in his latter days. He departed this life February 21st 1849 having been reduced to great distress. He was a jobber in cattle for many years.........he then became a butcher and used to kill the poor people's fat pigs, cut them up, and sell them for them. He died in an outhouse belonging to Noah Fake the carpenter. His family did not turn out well."*[67]

Through the records of the County Gaol[68], the Quarter Sessions[69] and a report in the Ipswich Journal,[70] we learn of the scrape that the 20 year old lacemaker Eliza Burrows got into. She was apprehended on the 21st April 1841 and charged with stealing a straw bonnet from the house of her parent's neighbour James Peck. The bonnet, which belonged to his daughter Mary Ann, was valued at five shillings. Eliza found herself incarcerated in Ipswich Gaol until her case finally came to trial in early July. I have little doubt that Eliza and her family were greatly relieved, when a verdict of *"No true bill"* was returned and she was duly discharged.

While amongst Yaxley's Parish Records a rather dramatic tale emerges from a newspaper cutting, probably kept by Revd. Sewell, because the transgressor was parishioner Henry Rockett, a 27 year old labourer, he was also the grandson of lacemaker Mary Rockett.

It was alleged that on the night of 6th December 1880, Rockett had broken into one of the Almshouses on Lambseth Street in Eye. It was the home of Ann Tuffs, an 80 year old widow and former lacemaker.

The prosecution claimed that he had entered into her home *"probably for the purpose of taking what he could lay his hands upon"* and in doing so woke her and a struggle ensued, during which *"she was hurt and one of her teeth was knocked out"*.

Fig.29 The Almshouses are the building on right hand side with the rather tall and ornate chimneys.

Her screams roused the neighbours and although by now her assailant had fled, he was identified by his hat left behind in the cottage.[71]

Revd. Sewell wrote to Henry Rockett's former regiment in hope of a character reference that might aid his case. However, the reply makes clear he would have been disappointed, for Rockett had been discharged from the Royal Marine Artillery the previous year, on account of his bad conduct.[72] When the case came to court, the Magistrates also took a rather dim view, for they sentenced him to twelve months imprisonment with hard labour.[73-74]

45

3. REDRAWING THE LACE

From the outset, I decided that it was important to remain as accurate to the original lace as possible and for this reason, I have resisted the temptation to improve a pattern. Working from digital photographs does have its advantages, enabling you to enlarge sections as and when needed, though occasionally the original sample was in a sad state, making it very difficult to determine its precise construction. In these instances, I have used my own judgement based on what I'd learnt from redrawing other patterns within the collection, while being mindful of retaining the patterns essence and integrity. It was important to establish the angle between the ground and footside as accurately as possible, it could range from between 52 to 60 degrees, but allowance for distortion also had to be taken into account; the lace is over 130 years old. All the patterns have been redrawn using the computer programme Lace R-XP by Il-Soft.

In the postcard of Mary Collins, it was just about possible to detect the footside being worked on the right hand side, and patterns 1249-1875.2 and 1249-1875.37 confirmed this to be the case. The design of both patterns requires the use of a non-continuous gimp thread, and closer inspection of the photographs clearly showed the cut ends protruding on one side of the lace. These gimp threads would have been cut as work progressed, allowing the bobbins to be used for subsequent repeats, they would have been cut with the uppermost side of the lace facing the lacemaker - this then indicates from which side and direction the lace should be viewed for determining where the footside lies.

*Fig. 30 Pattern
1249-1875.37*

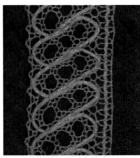

*Fig.31 Pattern
1250-1875.15*

Nearly all the original Suffolk samples had picots worked with just one or two twists making them rather loose, it didn't enhance their appearance, so I must confess that when re-working the samples, the picots were made with the more usual five twists. Although not all the Suffolk edgings have a picot headside, some are worked as snatch pins, with the working pair simply twisted around the pin.

Fewer twists for everything does seem to be the motto for Suffolk's lacemakers, though perhaps it is more a reflection on how they were taught. Their point ground stitch was frequently worked as half stitch and twist, rather than the more usual half stitch and two twists associated with Bucks Point. The footside was also regularly worked with fewer twists, but these variations have been adhered to when reworking the samples.

Point ground stitch was most frequently used for filling the main area of net, with honeycomb stitch used occasionally and one pattern, 1249-1875.34, incorporates kat stitch. Honeycomb stitch is also regularly used within many of the patterns motifs, along with the occasional appearance of mayflowers, half/cloth stitch diamonds and a sprinkling of tallies to decorate the ground.

A thicker gimp thread, is used as would be expected, for outlining and enhancing the pattern's design, though on occasion it has been used to work the headside fan, as in patterns 1249-1875.43 and 1250-1875.16. While in pattern 1249-1875.2, the gimp thread is used not just for outlining the oak leaf design but for filling it too. Another use for this thicker thread is the footside, where it may be paired with a finer thread and used as a passive.

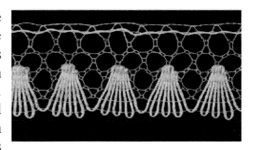

Fig.32 Pattern 1250-1875.16

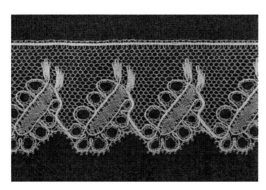

Fig.33 Pattern 1249-1875.16

The Suffolk lace patterns are predominantly geometric, but those numbered 1249-1875.2 and 1249-1875.16, flow more freely, with pin holes being positioned to meet the needs of the repeating oak leaf motifs. In the second pattern, two pairs of threads are carried with the gimp, transferring them from one motif to the next, though its design is a little clumsy. It seemed that the original lacemaker/s of both patterns had experienced difficulty in working them, for within the sections I had photographed, not a single pattern repeat was worked the same way twice in either sample. Having redrawn and worked both I was not particularly surprised!

One aspect of the construction of the Suffolk patterns, that seemed to differ quite significantly in comparison with other Point Ground laces, was in the formation of the valleys. In Bucks Point for example, the headside threads tend to curve round within the valley, but in the Suffolk patterns, the threads enter and leave the valley crossing through each other almost grid style, as can be seen in Figs. 34 & 35. There are of course always exceptions and slight variations, but on the whole the Suffolk patterns do tend to follow this method of working, although fifty four patterns is a small sample base to go by.

Having had the opportunity to look at a number of Lace Dealers' pattern books in museums both in England, Germany and Denmark, it still never ceases to amaze me how many and varied the patterns, within the Point Ground family of laces, actually are. A few of the Suffolk patterns are to be found in the repertoires of Bucks Point, Downton, Malmesbury and Devon Trolly laces.

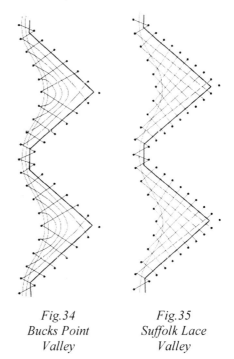

Fig.34
Bucks Point
Valley

Fig.35
Suffolk Lace
Valley

Two that particularly come to mind are known as 'The Grecian' and 'Princess', though not perfect matches, they are clearly from the same stable with their subtle variations. In the case of the Suffolk 'Grecian' pattern, 138-1883 the half stitch diamonds are grouped a little differently, while the cloth stitch trails in the Suffolk 'Princess' pattern, 1249-1875.15 are a little more rectangular.

Fig.36 Suffolk's 'Grecian' pattern
138-1883

Fig.37 Suffolk's 'Princess' pattern
1249-1875.15

The pattern 1250-1875.9, probably used for threading a ribbon through, is very similar to both a Malmesbury pattern known as 'The Egg', and one among a collection of work by lacemakers in Ipswich, Massachusetts.

In some cases, the slight differences that occur between similar pieces, can probably be attributed to the individual lacemaker's interpretation of a pattern. Three samples amongst the Suffolk collection (1249-1875.6; 1250-1875.10.1 and 1250-1875.10.2) ably demonstrate this, for they are quite clearly the same pattern, but each looks a little different. In each piece, the gimp work has been executed, consistently though slightly differently, within each of the three samples and leaves me in little doubt, that they are the work of three different lacemakers.

Personally, I feel that this particular regional lace shouldn't simply be dismissed because it's not as grand or as complex as some of its Point Ground cousins. Redrawing and working the Suffolk lace patterns has been a fascinating challenge, at times frustrating, but also very rewarding. The patterns are provided with working diagrams for you to copy for <u>your own personal</u> use and whichever techniques you decide to employ, I hope that you will enjoy working them.

* * * * *

Research into the county's lacemaking past will continue, for it has perhaps raised more questions than it has at present answered. It is also quite possible that there are still more bobbins waiting to be found, maybe even some patterns or pieces of lace, I would certainly be interested in knowing about them.

1249-1875.1

1249-1875.2

1249-1875.3

1249-1875.4

1249-1875.5

1249-1875.6

1249-1875.7

1249-1875.8

1249-1875.8D1

1249-1875.9

1249-1875.10

1249-1875.11

1249-1875.12

THE REWORKED SAMPLES OF SUFFOLK LACE

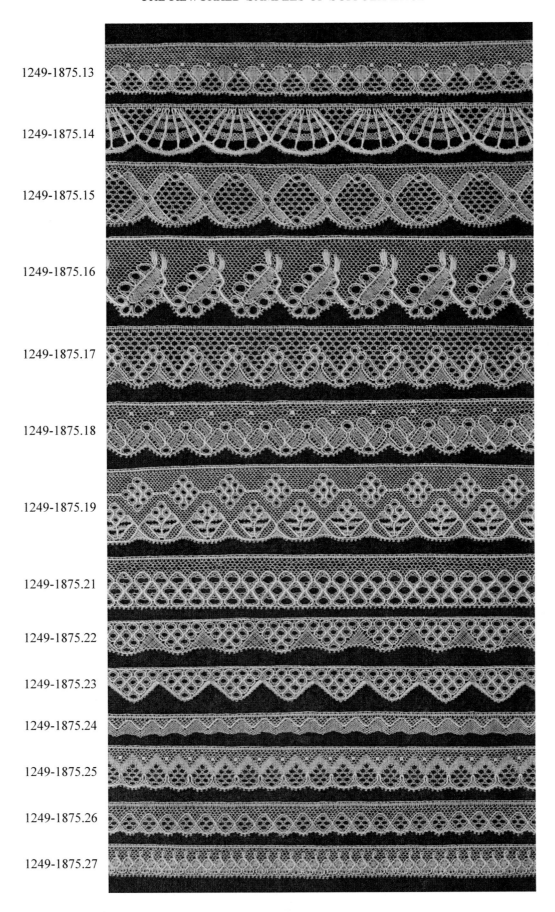

1249-1875.13

1249-1875.14

1249-1875.15

1249-1875.16

1249-1875.17

1249-1875.18

1249-1875.19

1249-1875.21

1249-1875.22

1249-1875.23

1249-1875.24

1249-1875.25

1249-1875.26

1249-1875.27

1249-1875.28

1249-1875.30

1249-1875.30

1249-1875.31

1249-1875.32

1249-1875.33

1249-1875.34

1249-1875.35

1249-1875.36

1249-1875.37

1249-1875.38

1249-1875.39

1249-1875.40

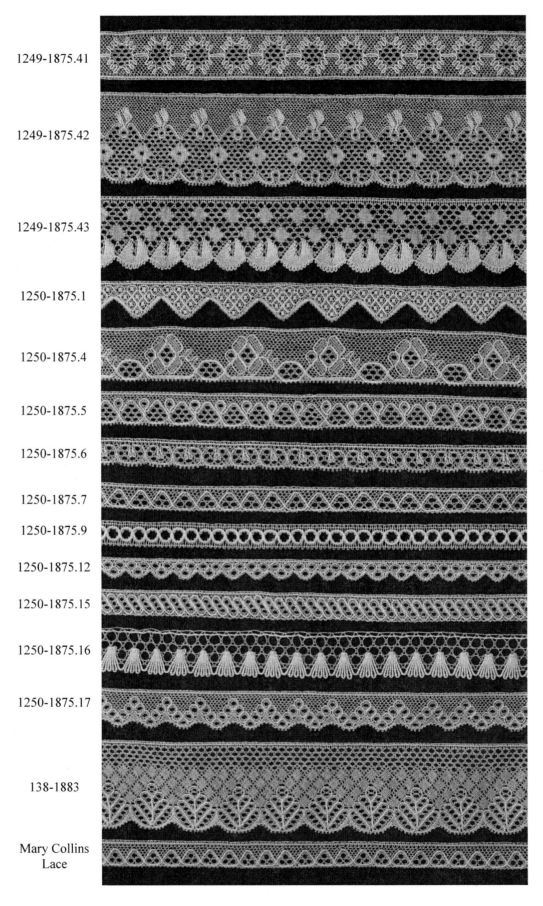

1249-1875.41

1249-1875.42

1249-1875.43

1250-1875.1

1250-1875.4

1250-1875.5

1250-1875.6

1250-1875.7

1250-1875.9

1250-1875.12

1250-1875.15

1250-1875.16

1250-1875.17

138-1883

Mary Collins
Lace

REFERENCES

1. Palliser, 1902, 4th Ed., p.394
2. Earnshaw, 1982, p.164
3. Blanchard, 1990, p.21
4. Ekwall, 1980, 4th Ed., p.171
5. Anon, c.1738
6. SROL Ipswich Journal
    10.2.1821 p.2(5)
7. Blome, 1673, p.213
8. Cox, 1730, vol.5, p.210
9. Anon, c.1738
10. Pinnock, 1818, p.36
11. Kirby, 1829, p.301
12. Pigot, 1830, p.99
13. Pigot, 1839, p.546
14. Kelly, 1858, p.599
15. Morris, 1868, p.175
16. Palliser, 1902, 4th Ed., p.394
17. Penderel Moody, 1909, p.21-22
18. Palliser, 1902, 4th Ed., p.394
19. Ibid, plate LXXXVII
20. Jourdain, 1908, p.102
21. Wright, 1924, p.84
22. Nevill Jackson, 1900, p.200
23. Head, 1922, p.96
24. Eirwen Jones, 1951, p.163
25. Nevill Jackson, 1900, p.200
26. Head, 1922, p.96
27. Penderel Moody, 1909, p.21
28. Penderel Moody, 1907, p.24
29. Sharpe, 1899, p.175
30. Hudson Moore, 1937, p.105
31. Penderel Moody, 1909, p.19-20
32. Eirwen Jones, 1951, p.163
33. Penderel Moody, 1909, p.21-22
34. Ibid, facing p.10
35. Webb, 1966, p.119
36. Ibid, 1966, p.135
37. Palliser, 1902, 4th Ed., p.294
38. Hudson Moore, 1937, p.14
39. Palliser, 1902, 4th Ed., p.294-5
40. Malster, 2000, p.69
41. Webb, 1966, p.15
42. Webb, 1966, p.15
43. Ibid, 1966, p.45
44. Levey, 1983, p.27
45. Baker, D, 2007
46. Hudson Moore, 1937, p.90
47. Yallop, 1992, p.18
48. Ibid, p.12-22
49. Spenceley, 1973, p.90
50. Levey, 1983, p.28
51. Ibid, p.28
52. Penderel Moody, 1909, p.7-8
53. Levey, 1983, p.59
54. Blome, 1673, p.212
55. Dymond & Northeast,
    1985, p.66-67
56. Huetson, 1973, p.58
57. Palliser, 1902, 4th Ed., p.394
58. Penderel Moody, 1909, p.21
59. Lace, 1982, No:26, p.16
60. Stanbury, 2006, p.87
61. Letters, various
62. SROI. FB128 L5/2-3
63. Ibid. FB 128 A1/17
64. Ibid. FB 128 L5/7
65. SROL Ipswich Journal
    10.02.1821 p.2(5)
66. Penderel Moody, 1909, p.21
67. Cobbold, 1977, p.132
68. SROI Gaol Records,
    1841, J465 609/31/p.378
69. SROI Quarter Sessions,
    1841, p.421
70. SROL Ipswich Journal,
    10.07.1841 4(6)
71. SROL PR's Yaxley,
    FB128 Fiche10 of 11
72. SROL PR's Yaxley,
    FB128 Fiche 10 of 11
73. SROI Quarter Sessions
    1881, p197
74. SROI Gaol Records
    1881, B105/2/115

GLOSSARY

It is easy to forget that not everyone reading this book will necessarily be a lacemaker, so for those unfamiliar with the crafts jargon I have included a brief, but simple, glossary. They are not exhaustive explanations but are given in context with the terms used in this book. Some of the terms listed describe elements within the patterns themselves and examples are given. I would also highly recommend Alexandra Stillwell's *Illustrated Dictionary of Lacemaking* for further reference.

* * * * *

CATCH PIN   A technique used in Point Ground lace. The pin is placed either to the right or left side of a pair rather than between them, making a firmer stitch, used adjacent to the footside and also vertical gimps.

CLOTH STITCH   One of the two basic stitches for making lace. When worked it looks like a piece of even weave fabric.

DIAMOND   A small area bounded by a diamond of pinholes worked in either cloth stitch (see pattern 1249-1875.29) or half stitch (see pattern 1249-1875.6)

EDGING   A strip of lace with both a decorative headside and a footside that is designed to be attached to a piece of fabric (see pattern 1249-1875.10).

FOOTSIDE   The edge that is used for stitching a strip of lace to fabric.

GIMP   The thicker or coarser thread integral to the formation of the pattern's design and often used to outline or highlight a motif (see pattern 1249-1875.8). It plays no part in forming the stitches but simply passes between pairs of threads which are in turn twisted on either side of it. It is sometimes used to weave through pairs to work a fan (see pattern 1249-1875.43) or to fill an area within the design (see pattern 1249-1875.2).

GROUND   The area of lace that acts as a background to the overall design. Frequently worked in point ground stitch, but also worked in honeycomb stitch and kat stitch.

HALF STITCH   One of the two basic stitches used for making lace, it is more open than cloth stitch.

HEADSIDE   The decorative often undulating side of an edging. It is usually decorated with picots, but occasionally a snatch pin is worked instead.

HONEYCOMB   A decorative stitch used as a ground stitch (see pattern 1249-1875.17), also used as a filling within the pattern and/or to form rings that are outlined by a gimp thread (see pattern 1249-1875.40).

INSERTION A strip of lace that has two footsides, allowing both edges to be attached to fabric (see pattern 1249-1875.33).

KAT STITCH One of the ground stitches used in Point Ground lace (see pattern 1249-1875.34).

MAYFLOWER A decorative cloth stitch diamond worked in an area of honeycomb stitch (see pattern 1249-1875.33)

PASSIVE/S The threads that run down alongside the footside and also the headside, usually one or two pairs.

PICOT A small loop that decorates the headside edge.

POINT GROUND LACE A specific group of laces that includes Bucks Point, Devon Trolly, Downton, Lille, Malmesbury and Suffolk and is characterised by its style. The patterns are designed on a grid having an angle of between 52 and 70 degrees.

POINT GROUND The most frequently worked background stitch which forms a delicate mesh or net ground.

PRICKING A card or parchment pattern with a series of pinholes. Pins are inserted to support the threads while making the lace.

SNATCH PIN The worker threads are twisted and pass around the headside pin and then re-enter the main body of the work. No picot is formed (see pattern 1249-1875.39).

SPANGLE A ring of beads attached by wire to the base of an East Midlands bobbin. They add weight and aid tension. They do not help to identify which bobbin/s are used for working the pattern.

TALLY/TALLIES A square shaped spot. It is made by weaving one thread back and forth across three threads. Used most often to decorate the area of ground within a design (see pattern 1249-1875.39).

TRAIL A band of cloth stitch or half stitch that zigzags through the design (see pattern 1249-1875.25).

TROLLY (LACE) A term of Flemish origin and once given to a group of English laces that resembled the Flemish Trolle Kant grounds. Also sometimes used to describe the coarse outlining thread.

WORKERS A pair of bobbins woven across each row when making cloth and/or half stitch.

BIBLIOGRAPHY

Anon, *The New General English Dictionary*, c.1738

Blanchard, Joan, *Malmesbury Lace*, (Batsford) 1990

Blome, Richard, *Britannia*, (Tho. Rycroft London) 1673

Bullock, Alice-May, *Lace and Lacemaking*, (Batsford) 1981

Canning, Shelley, *32 Downton Lace Patterns*, (Canning) ——

Cobbold, Revd. Richard, *The Biography of a Victorian Village*, (Batsford) 1977

Cotterell Raffel, Marta, *The Laces of Ipswich*,
                  (University Press of New England) 2003

Cox, Revd. Thomas, *Magna Britannia Suffolk*, (E & R Nutt) 1730

Dymond, David & Northeast, Peter, *A History of Suffolk*,
                  (Phillimore & Co. Ltd.) 1985

Earnshaw, Pat., *A Dictionary of Lace*, (Shire Publications) 1982

Eirwen Jones, Mary, *The Romance of Lace*, (Spring Books) ——

Ekwall, Eilert, *The Concise Oxford Dictionary of English Place-names*,
                  (Oxford University Press) 4th Edition 1980

Gwynne, Judyth L., *The Illustrated Dictionary of Lace* (Batsford) 1997

Head, Mrs R.E., *The Lace and Embroidery Collector - A Guide to Old Lace &*
                  Embroidery, (Jenkins) 1921

Hudson Moore, N., *The Lace Book*, (Tudor Publishing Co.) 1937

Huetson, T.L., *Lace and Bobbins: A History and Collector's Guide*,
                  (A.S. Barnes & Co.,) 1973

Jourdain, Margaret, *Old Lace - A Handbook for Collectors*,
                  (Batsford facsimile of 1908 Edition) 1988

Kemp, Bertha, *Downton Lace*, (Dryad Press Ltd) 1988

Kirby, John, *The Suffolk Traveller*, (J. Munro Woodbridge) 1829

Levey, Santina M., *Lace - A History*, (Victoria & Albert Museum) 1983

Malster, Robert, *A History of Ipswich*, (Phillimore & Co. Ltd.) 2000

McFadzean, Carol, *Devon Trolly Lace - The lost lace of the East Devon Coast*,
                  (C. McFadzean) 2004

Nevill Jackson, Mrs F. & E. Jesurum, *A History of Hand-Made Lace*,
                  (L. Upcott Gill, London) 1900

Page, William, (Editor), *The Victoria History of the County of Suffolk*,
                  (Constable & Co.) 1907

Paine, Clive, *The History of Eye*, (Benyon de Beauvoir) 1993

Palliser, Mrs F.M. Bury, *History of Lace*, 1st Edition 1865; 2nd 1869; 3rd 1875 &
                  4th 1902

Penderel Moody, Miss A., *Devon Pillow Lace. Its History and How to Make It*,
                  (Cassell & Co. Ltd.) 1907

Penderel Moody, Miss A., *Lace Making and Collecting. An Elementary Handbook*,
                  (Cassell & Co. Ltd.) 1909

Pinnock, Samuel, *History & Topography of* Suffolk, (——), 1818

Reigate, Emily, *An Illustrated Guide to Lace*, (Antique Collectors' Club) 1986

Riley, Kate, *Bucks Point Prickings*, (The Lace Guild) 1999

Sharpe, A. Mary, *Point and Pillow Lace*, (John Murray) 1899

Short, Mary, *Historical Reminiscences of Eye*, (Comer & Phillips) 1922
Spenceley, G.F.R., *The Origins of the English Pillow Lace Industry*,
        (Agricultural History Review, XXI), 1973
Skovgaard, Inge, *The Technique of Tønder Lace*, (Batsford) 1991
Sortwell, H.T., *Geography of the County of Suffolk*, (Wm. Collins Sons & Co.)
Stillwell, Alexandra, *Illustrated Dictionary of Lacemaking*,
        (Cassell Publishers Ltd.) 1996
Webb, J. (ed.), *Poor Relief in Elizabethan Ipswich*,
        (Suffolk Records Society Volume IX) 1996
Wright, Thomas, *The Romance of the Lace Pillow*, (Armstrong) 1924
Yallop, H.J., *The History of the Honiton Lace Industry*,
        (University of Exeter Press) 1992

OTHER SOURCES
(ARTICLES, BOOKLETS, DIRECTORIES, LECTURES, LETTERS)

Baker, Douglas, *The Decline of the Wool & the Rise of the Silk*, (Lecture) 2008
Caulton, Geoff, *Suffolk Lace*, Lace (Lace Guild) April 1982, Number 26
Diss Express, March 1988
East Anglian Daily Times, June & October 1981
Ipswich Journal, 1821
Kelly's Post Office Directories - Suffolk 1858, London 1843-1875
Lauridsen, Inger, *Lace Dealers and Their Travels*, (Lecture) 2007
Letters - relating to the Misses Wright Collection in the author's possession
McFadzean, Carol, *Devon Trolly Lace*, (Lectures) 2006 & 2007
Morris's Suffolk Directory, 1868
Parry, Pompi, *Downton Lace*, (Lecture) 2007
Pigot's Directories, 1830 & 1839
OIDFA Study Group, *Point Ground Lace, A Comparative Study*, (OIDFA), 2000
Rixon, Angharad, *Just a piece of lace?* (The Bulletin of the Australasian Institute for
        Maritime Archaeology) 2002 Vol. 26
Stanbury, Myra, *Unfurling the secret of the Batavia lace and lace bobbins*, chapter
        from *Dutch Connections: 400 years of Australian-
        Dutch maritime links 1606-2006*, (Australian National
        Maritime Museum) 2006
Stang, Marianne, *Point Ground Laces*, (Lecture) 2007

The Lace
Patterns

Mary Collins Lace

Bobbins 13 pairs

Thread Brok 120/2

Gimp DMC Coton á Broder 16
1 pair

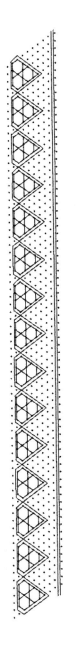

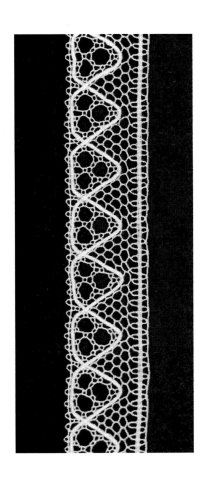

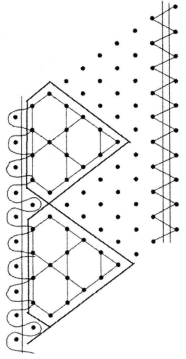

Pattern 1249-1875.10

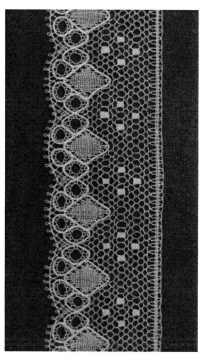

Bobbins 25 pairs

Thread Brok 120/2

Gimp DMC Coton á Broder 25
1 pair

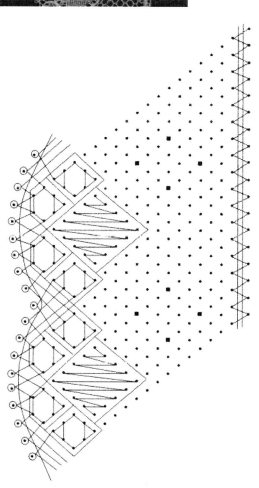

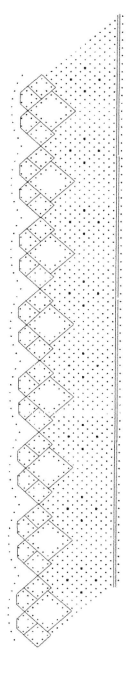

Pattern 1249-1875.1

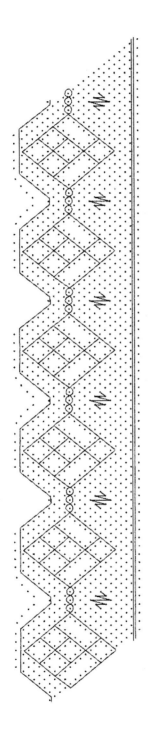

Bobbins 27 pairs

Thread Brok 120/2

Gimp DMC Coton á Broder 25
1 pair + 1 single bobbin

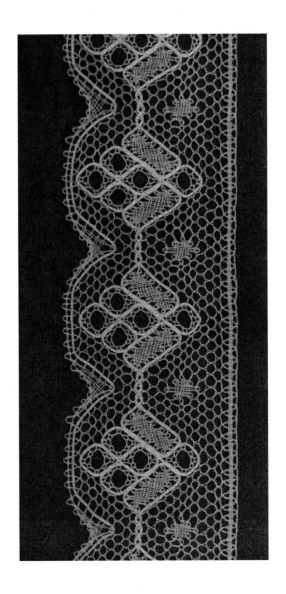

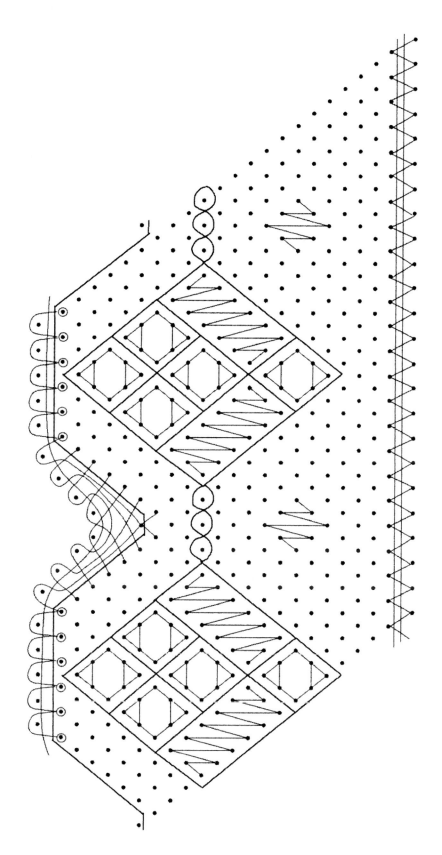

nb. ringed pinholes are best
worked as catch pins

63

Pattern 1249-1875.2

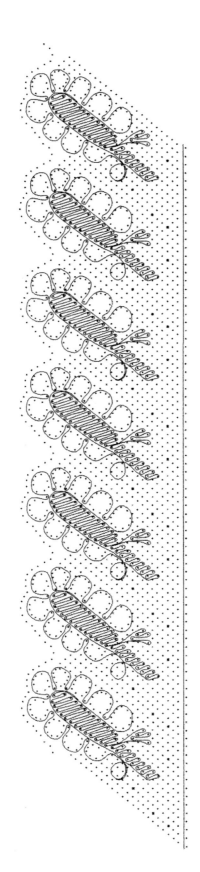

Bobbins 34 pairs

Thread   Brok 120/2

Gimp   DMC Coton á Broder 25
         1 pair + 1 single bobbin

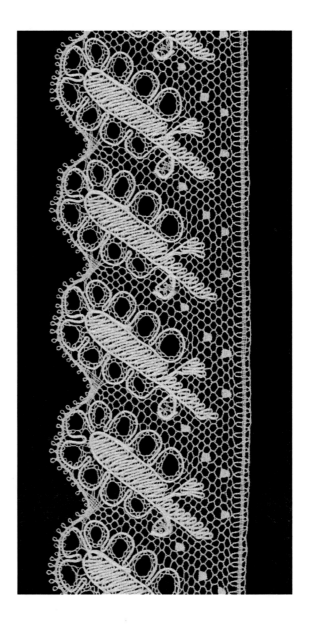

64

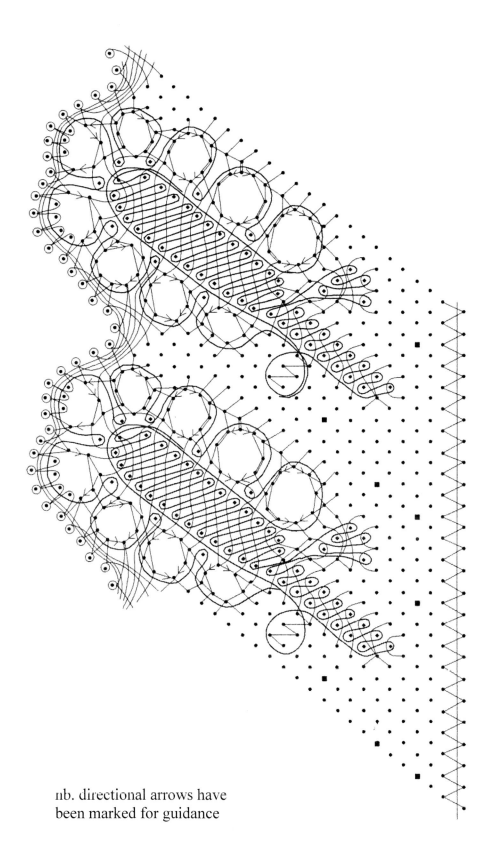

nb. directional arrows have
been marked for guidance

65

Pattern 1249-1875.6

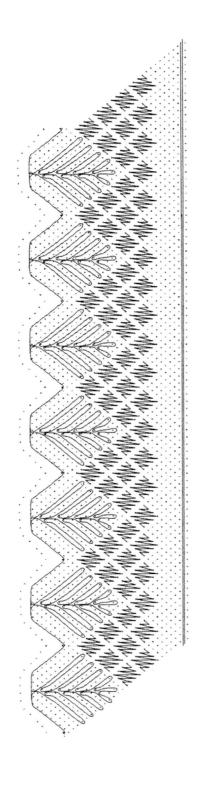

Bobbins 39 pairs

Thread Brok 120/2

Gimp DMC Coton á Broder 25
1 pair + 1 single bobbin

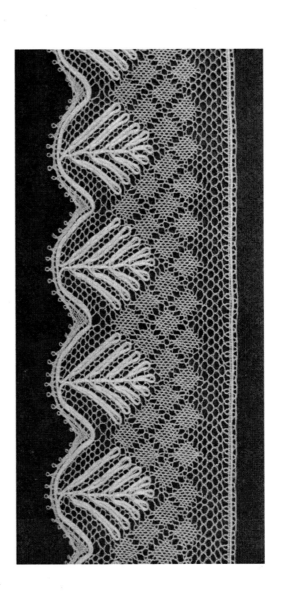

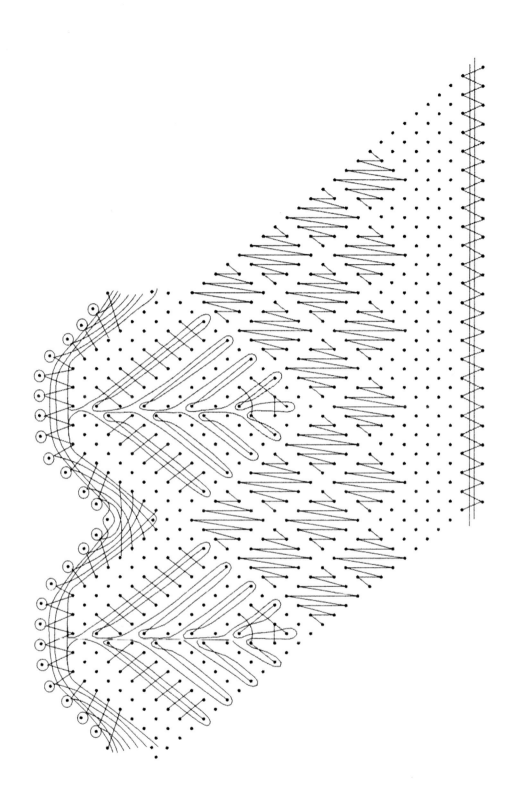

Pattern 1249-1875.8

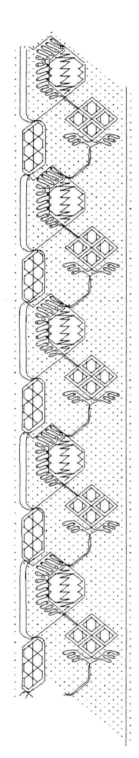

Bobbins 27 pairs (1 bobbin DMC 25)

Thread Brok 120/2

Gimp DMC Coton á Broder 25
2 pairs + 1 single bobbin

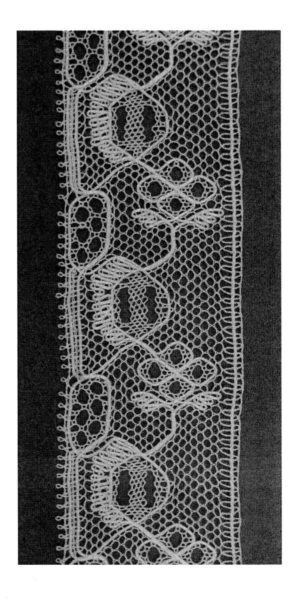

68

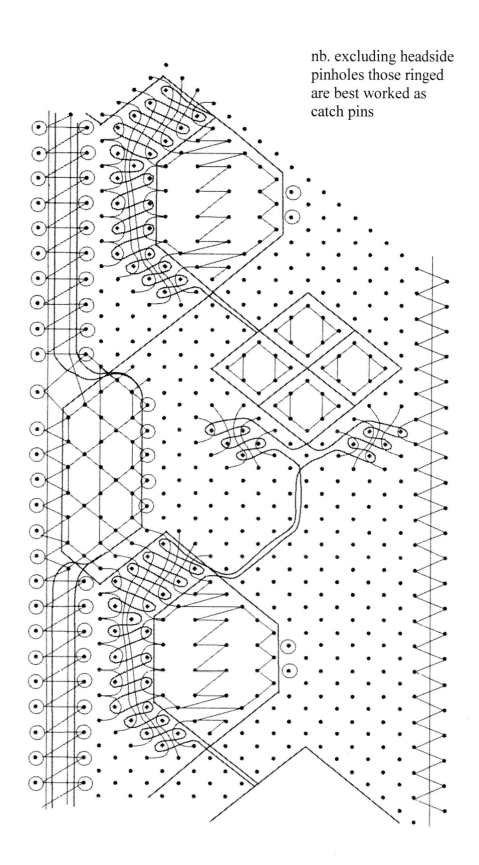

nb. excluding headside
pinholes those ringed
are best worked as
catch pins

69

Pattern 1249-1875.8D1

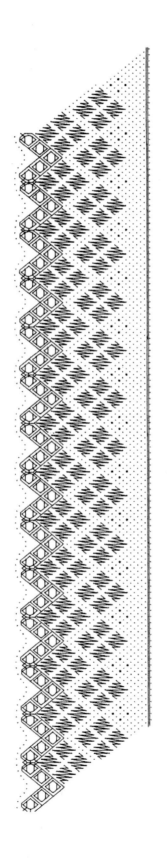

Bobbins 39 pairs

Thread Brok 120/2

Gimp DMC Coton á Broder 25
1 pair

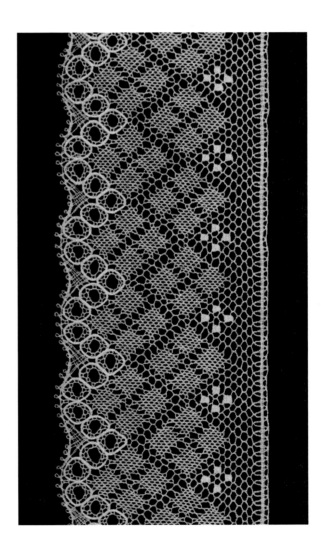

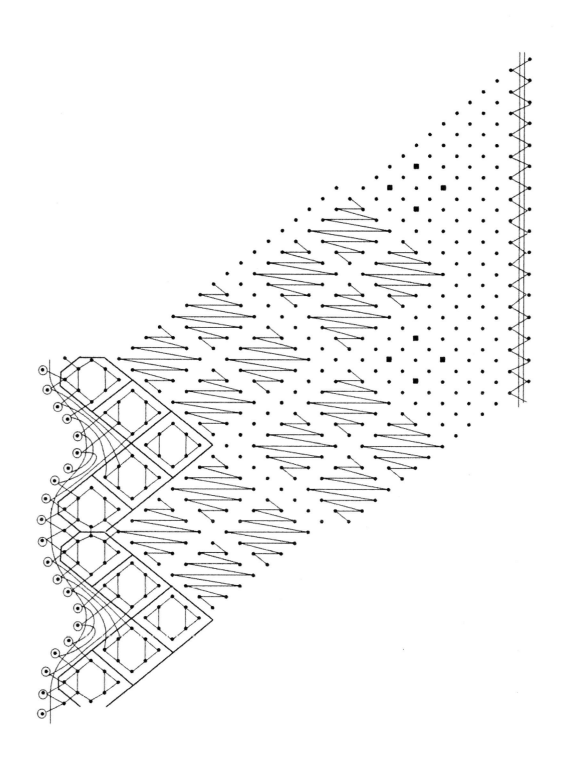

71

Pattern 1249-1875.9

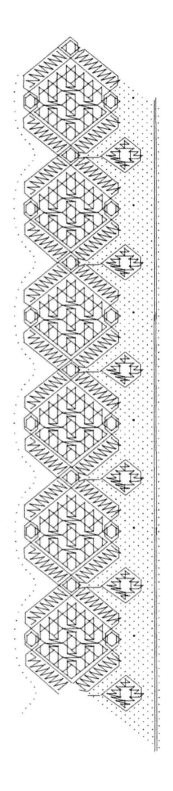

Bobbins 35 pairs

Thread   Brok 120/2

Gimp   DMC Coton á Broder 25
2 pairs

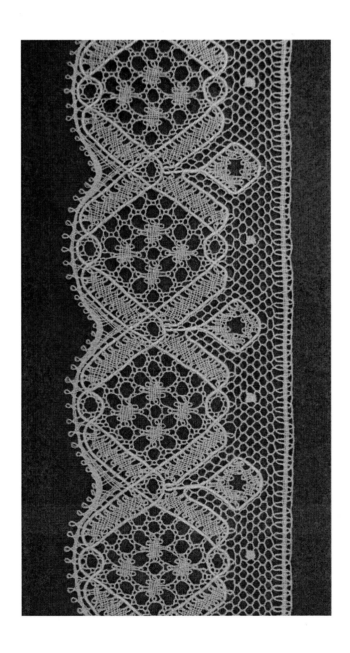

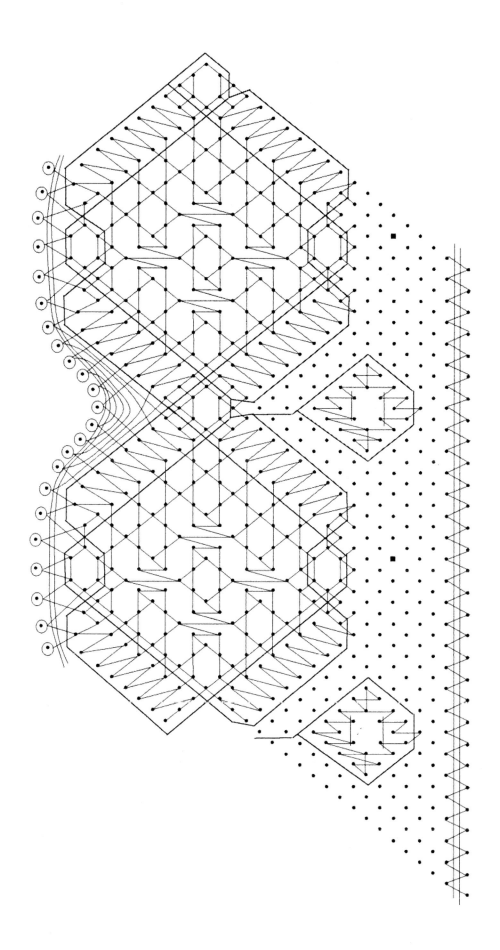

Pattern 1249-1875.11

Bobbins 18 pairs

Thread Brok 120/2

Gimp DMC Coton á Broder 16
2 single bobbins

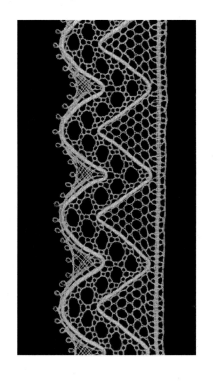

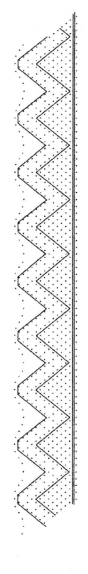

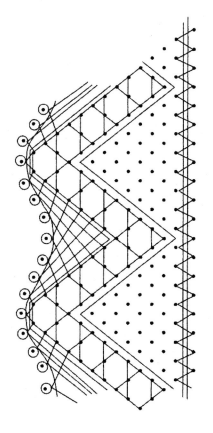

Pattern 1249-1875.13

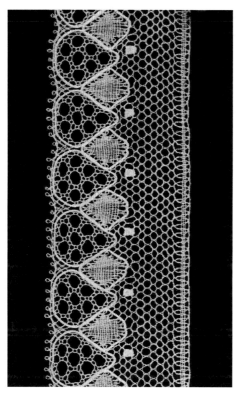

Bobbins 25 pairs + 1 single bobbin

Thread   Brok 120/2

Gimp   DMC Coton á Broder 25
1 pair

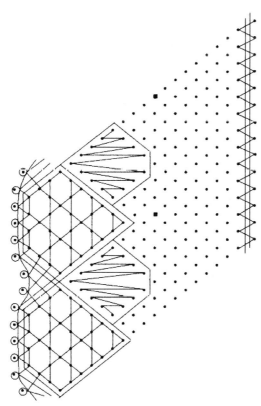

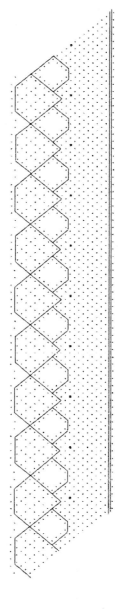

Pattern 1249-1875.14

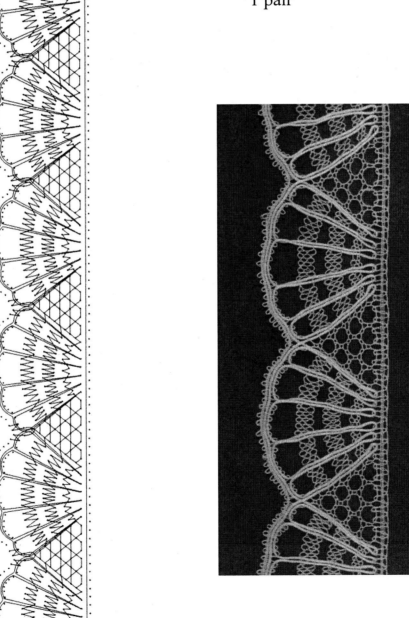

Bobbins 15 pairs + 1 single bobbin

Thread Brok 120/2

Gimp DMC Coton á Broder 25
1 pair

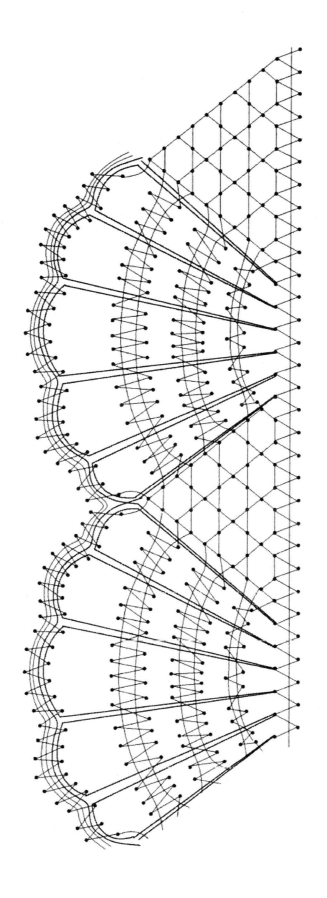

77

Pattern 1249-1875.16

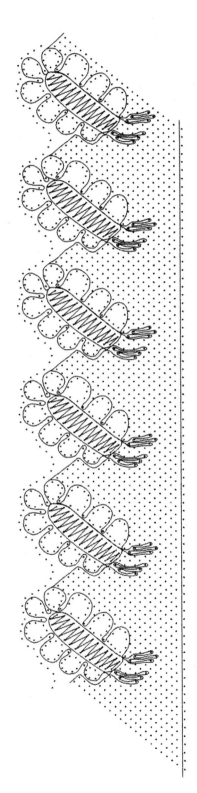

Bobbins 31 pairs (1 bobbin DMC 25)

Thread   Brok 120/2

Gimp   DMC Coton á Broder 16
           2 pairs + 1 single bobbin

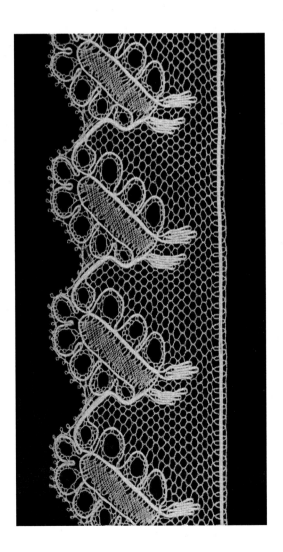

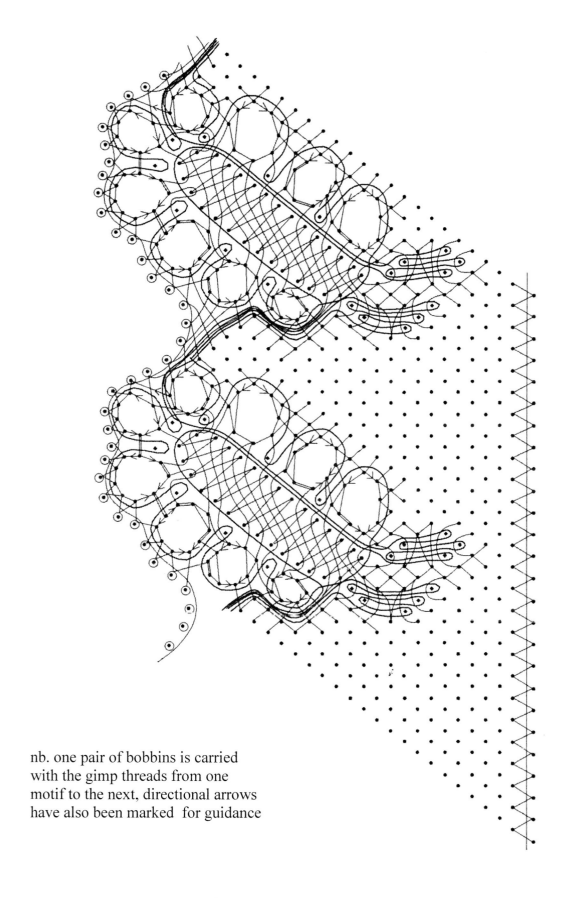

nb. one pair of bobbins is carried
with the gimp threads from one
motif to the next, directional arrows
have also been marked for guidance

Pattern 1249-1875.17

Bobbins 27 pairs

Thread Brok 120/2

Gimp DMC Coton á Broder 25
1 pair

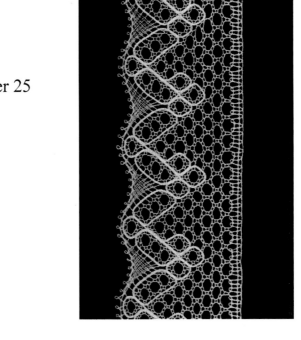

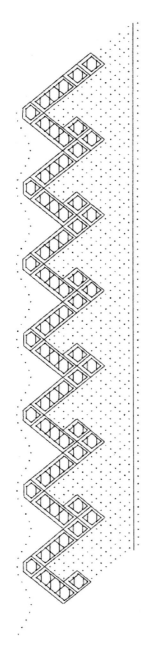

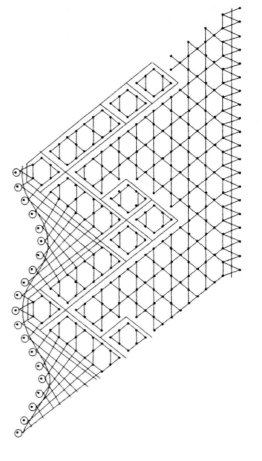

Pattern 1249-1875.18

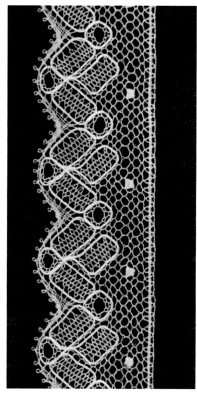

Bobbins 25 pairs

Thread   Brok 120/2

Gimp   DMC Coton á Broder 25
             1 pair

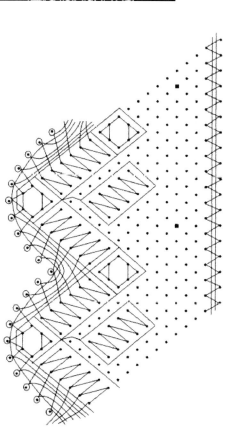

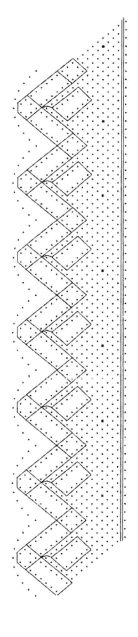

81

Pattern 1249-1875.19

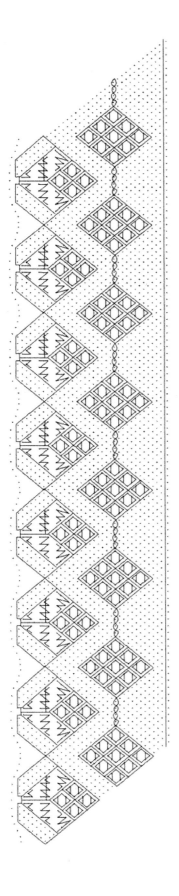

Bobbins 39 pairs

Thread Brok 120/2

Gimp DMC Coton á Broder 25
3 pairs

82

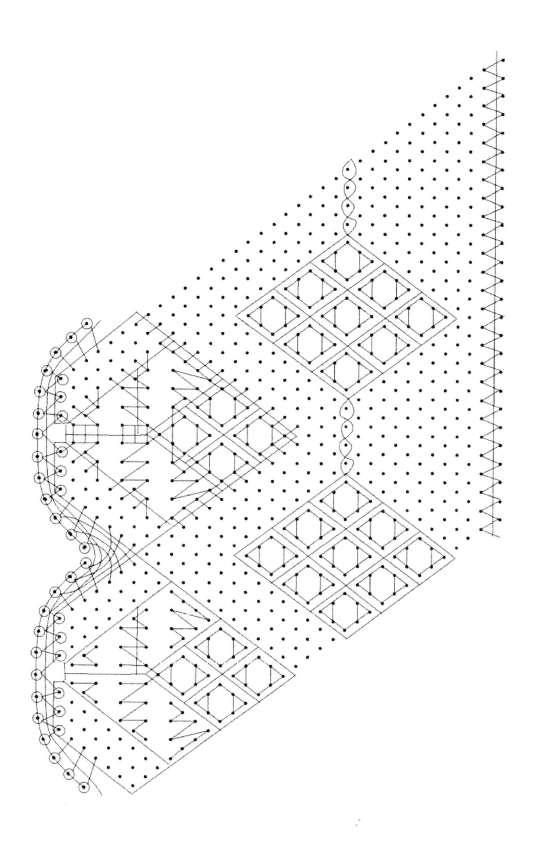

Pattern 1249-1875.23

Bobbins 16 pairs

Thread Brok 120/2

Gimp DMC Coton á Broder 25
1 pair

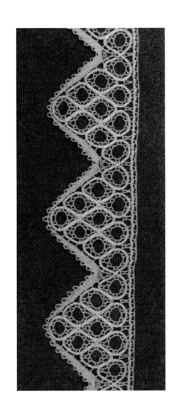

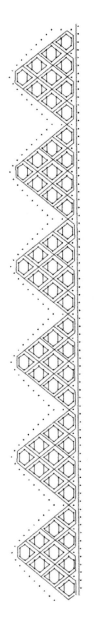

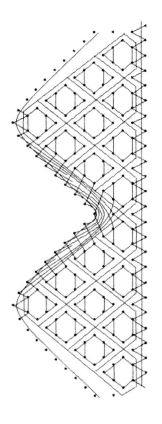

Pattern 1249-1875.25

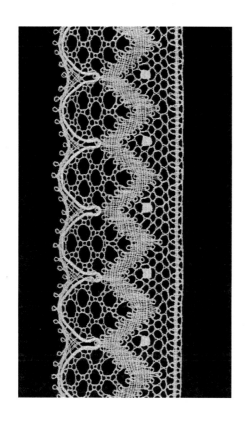

Bobbins 24 pairs

Thread   Brok 120/2

Gimp   DMC Coton á Broder 25
1 single bobbin

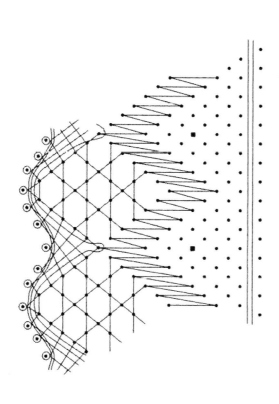

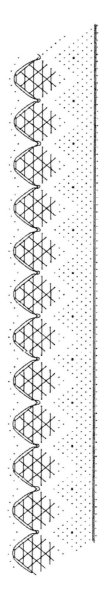

Pattern 1249-1875.27

Bobbins 17 pairs

Thread   Brok 120/2

Gimp   DMC Coton á Broder 25
           1 pair

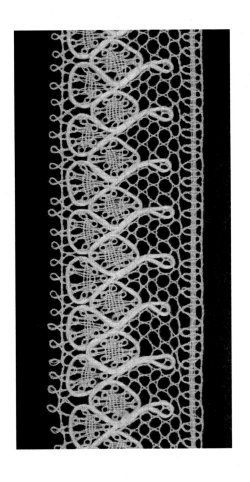

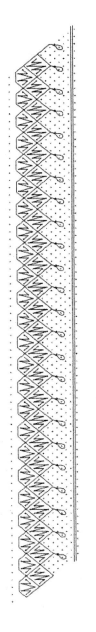

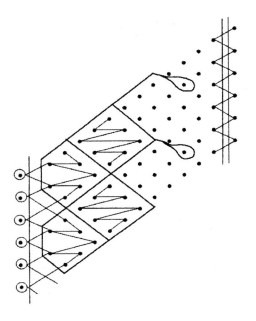

Pattern 1249-1875.28

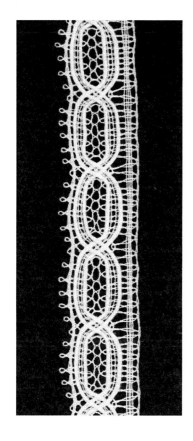

Bobbins 11 pairs

Thread Brok 120/2

Gimp DMC Coton á Broder 16
2 pairs

nb. ringed pinholes are best worked as
catch pins

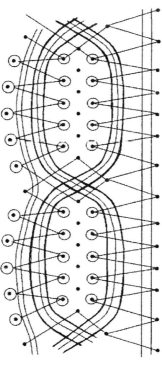

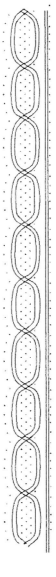

Pattern 1249-1875.29

Bobbins 19 pairs

Thread Brok 120/2

Gimp DMC Coton á Broder 16
1 single bobbin

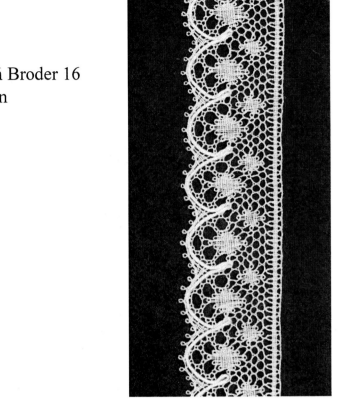

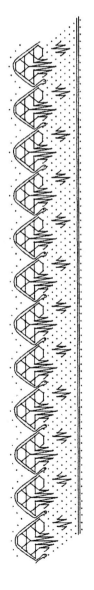

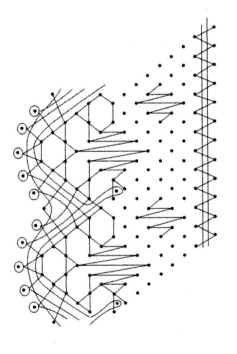

Pattern 1249-1875.30

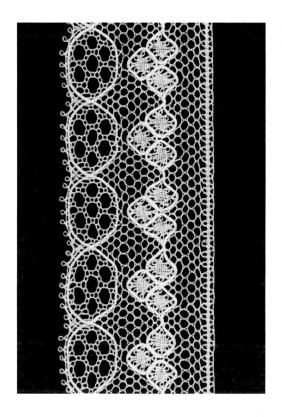

Bobbins 27 pairs

Thread Brok 120/2

Gimp DMC Coton á Broder 25
2 pairs

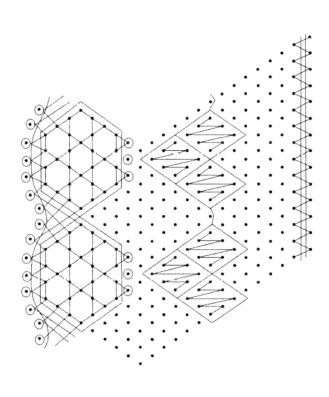

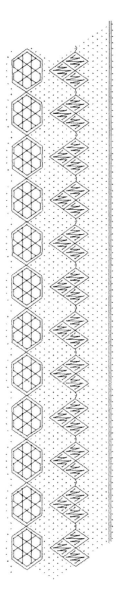

89

Pattern 1249-1875.33

Bobbins 29 pairs + 2 single bobbins

Thread Brok 120/2

Gimp DMC Coton á Broder 25
2 pairs

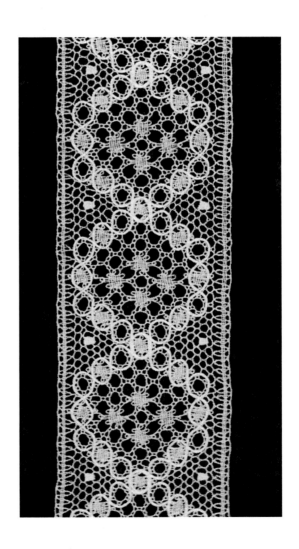

90

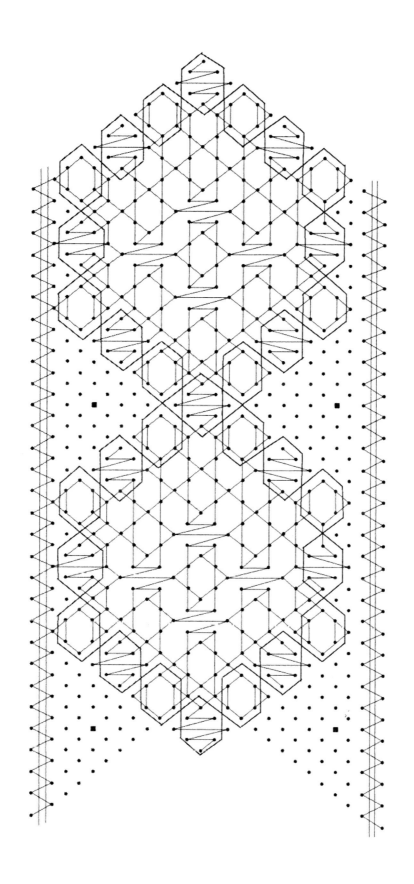

Pattern 1249-1875.34

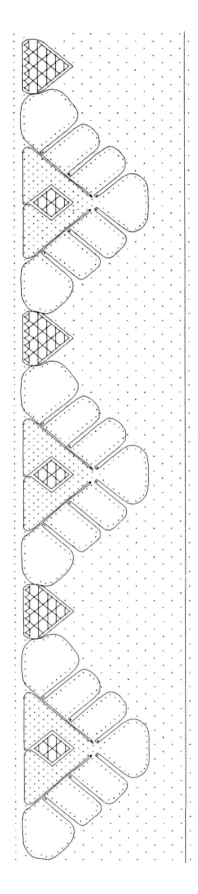

Bobbins 41 pairs

Thread Brok 120/2

Gimp DMC Coton á Broder 16
1 pair

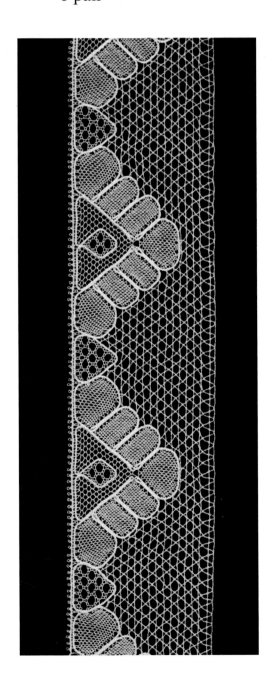

92

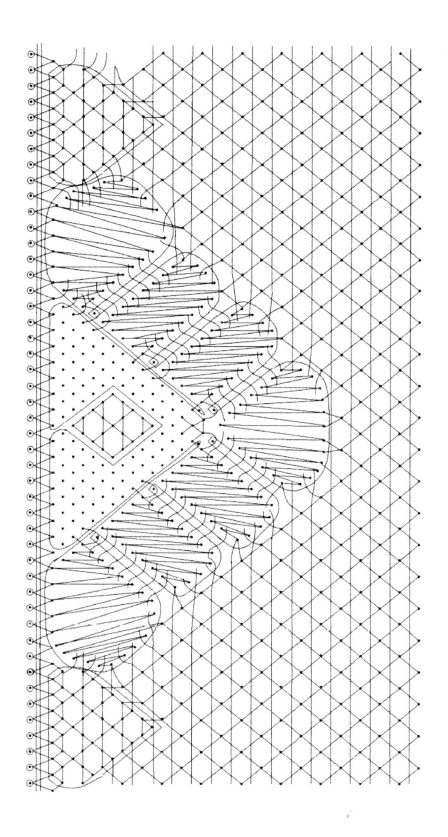

93

Pattern 1249-1875.35

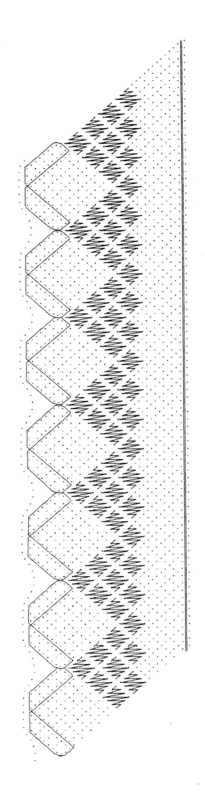

Bobbins 42 pairs

Thread Brok 120/2

Gimp DMC Coton á Broder 25
1 pair

94

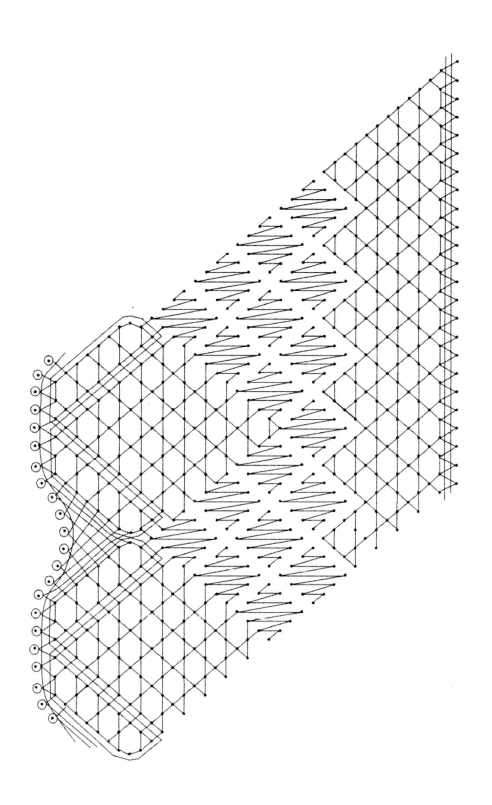

Pattern 1249-1875.37

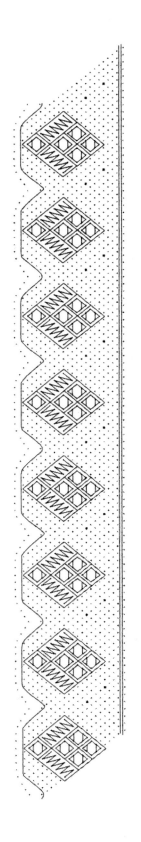

Bobbins 28 pairs

Thread Brok 120/2

Gimp DMC Coton á Broder 25
1 pair & 1 single bobbin

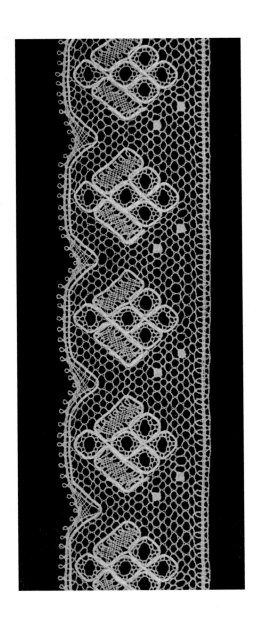

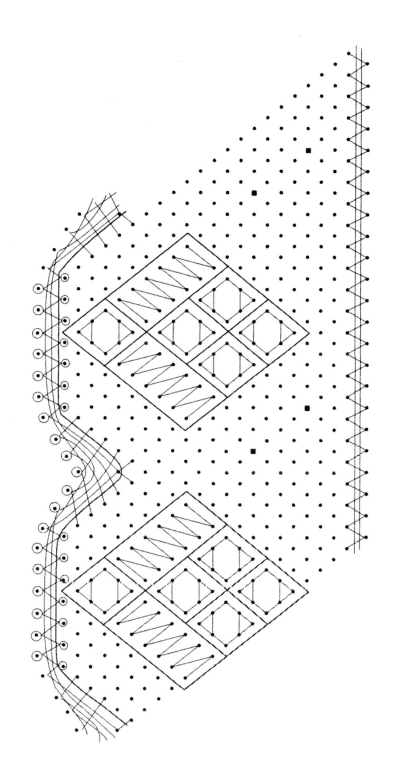

Pattern 1249-1875.39

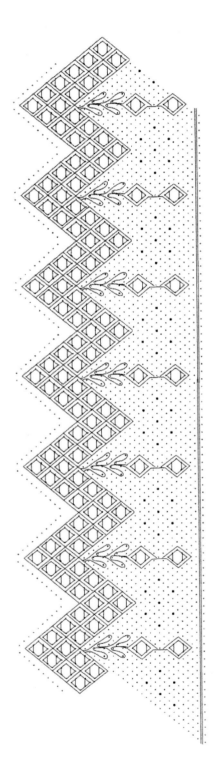

Bobbins 42 pairs

Thread Brok 120/2

Gimp DMC Coton á Broder 25
1 pair

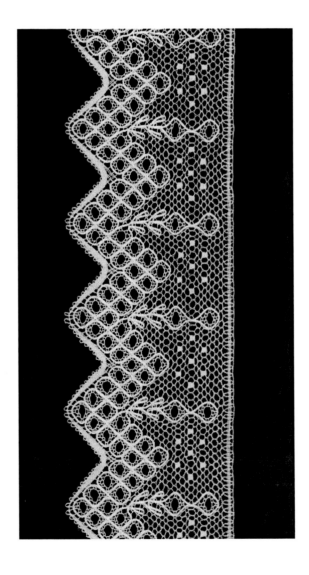

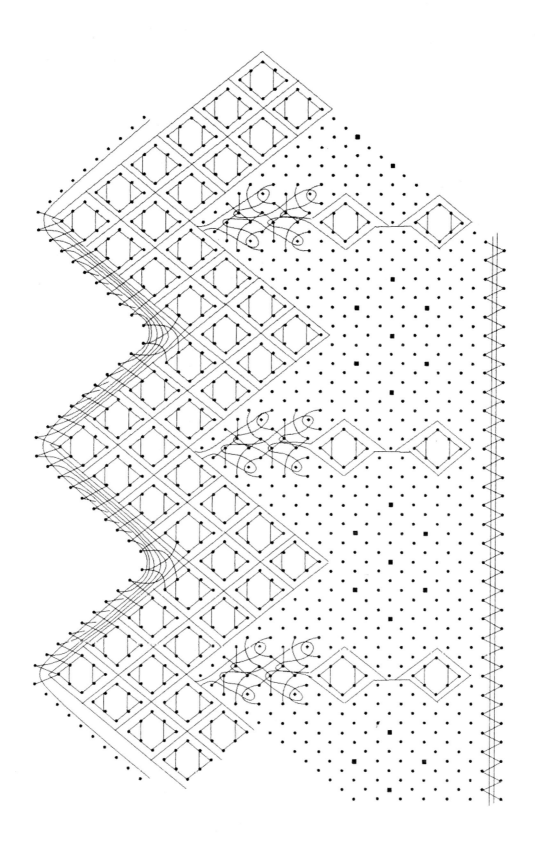

Pattern 1249-1875.40

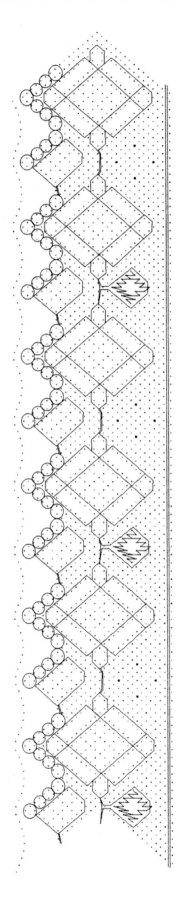

Bobbins 36 pairs

Thread Brok 120/2

Gimp DMC Coton á Broder 25
3 pairs

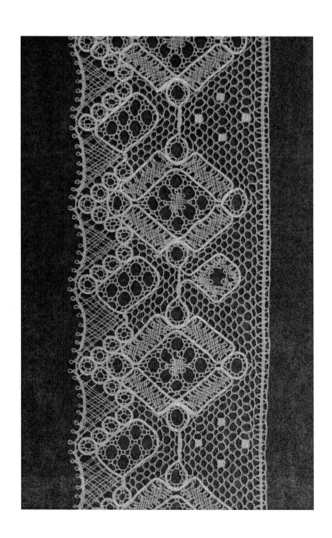

100

nb. an arrow indicates that a gimp
is added at this point for the
centre of each pattern repeat

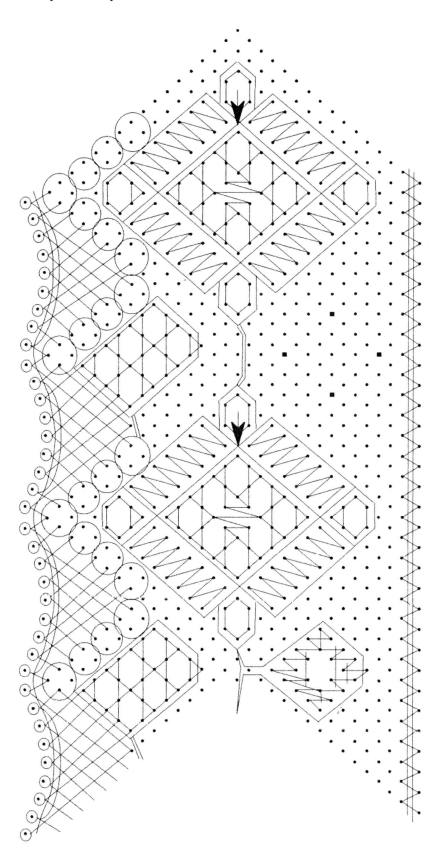

101

Pattern 1249-1875.31

Bobbins 18 pairs + 2 single bobbins

Thread Brok 120/2

Gimp DMC Coton á Broder 16
1 pair

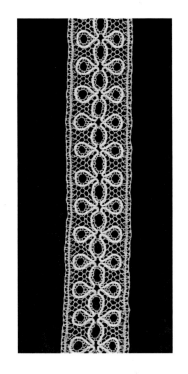

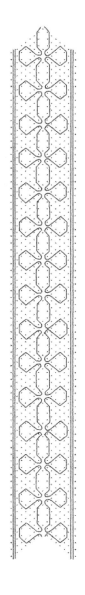

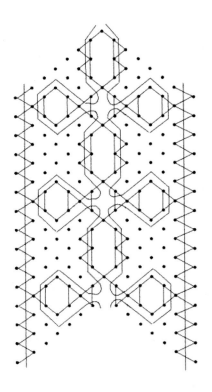

Pattern 1249-1875.41

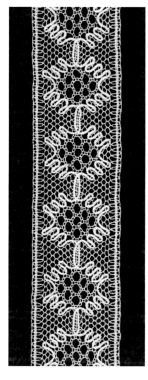

Bobbins 26 pairs

Thread Brok 120/2

Gimp DMC Coton á Broder 16
1 pair

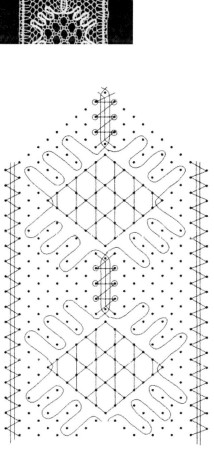

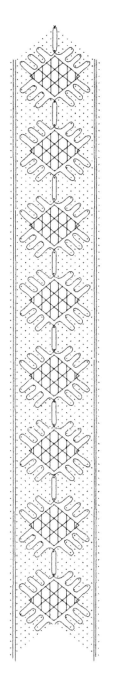

Pattern 1249-1875.42

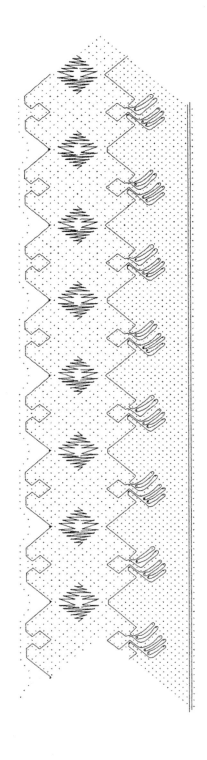

Bobbins 46 pairs + 1 single bobbin

Thread Brok 120/2

Gimp DMC Coton á Broder 25
2 single bobbins

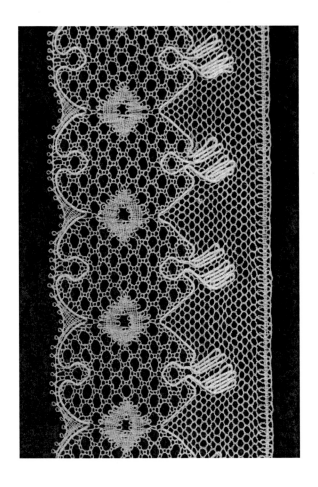

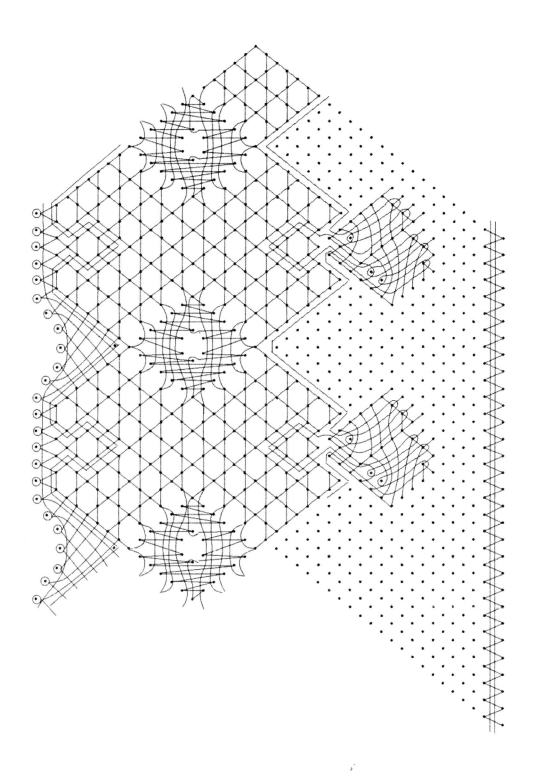

Pattern 1249-1875.43

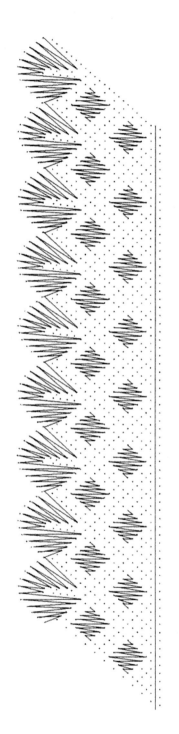

Bobbins 28 pairs + 1 single bobbin

Thread Brok 120/2

Gimp DMC Coton á Broder 25
1 single bobbin

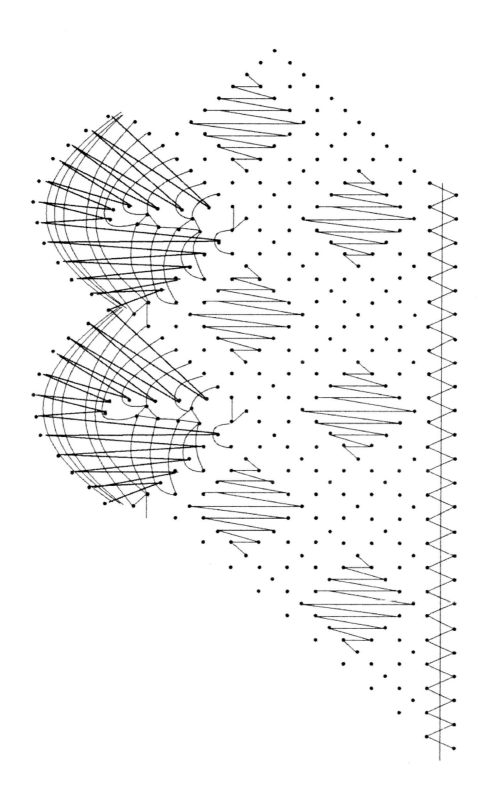

Pattern 1249-1875.36

Bobbins 27 pairs

Thread Brok 120/2

Gimp DMC Coton á Broder 25
1 pair

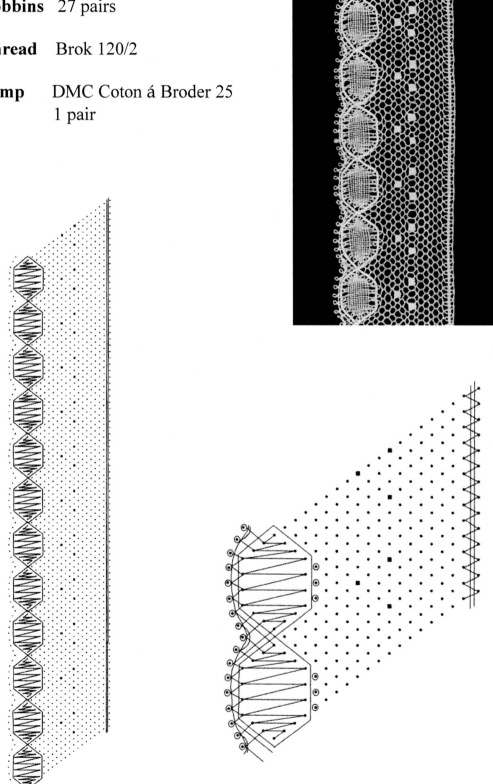

Pattern 1250-1875.1

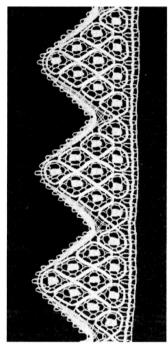

Bobbins 16 pairs

Thread Brok 120/2

Gimp DMC Coton á Broder 25
1 pair

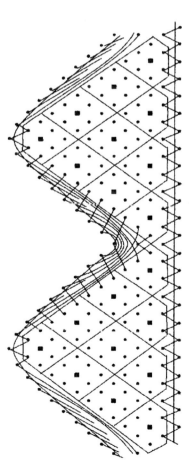

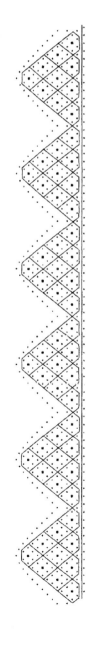

Pattern 1250-1875.4

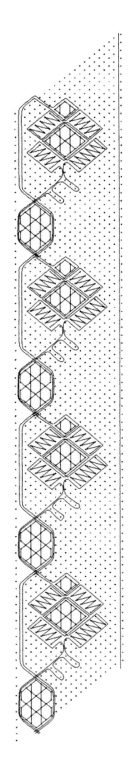

Bobbins 24 pairs

Thread Brok 120/2

Gimp DMC Coton á Broder 25
2 pairs

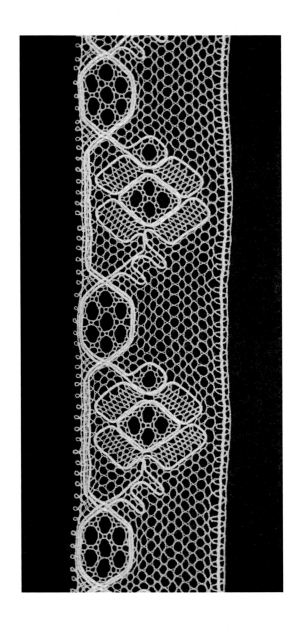

110

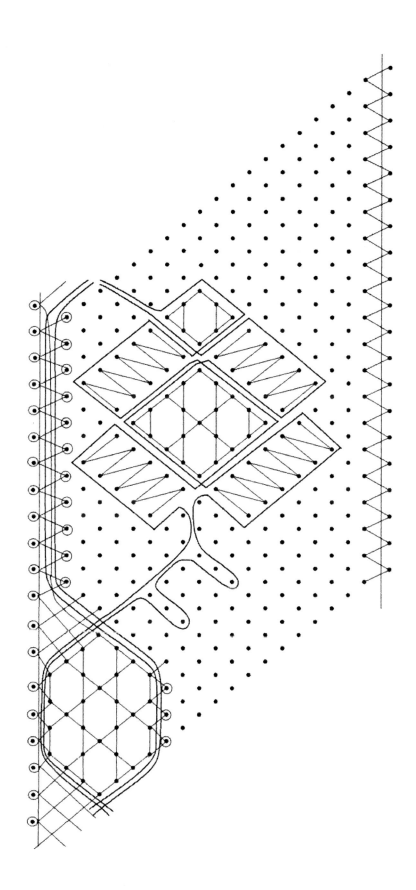

Pattern 1250-1875.5

Bobbins 17 pair (1 bobbin DMC 16)

Thread Brok 120/2

Gimp DMC Coton á Broder 16
1 pair

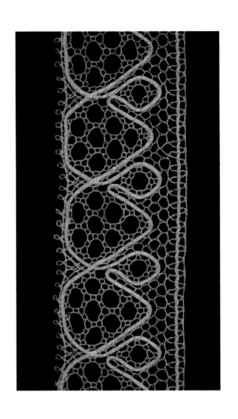

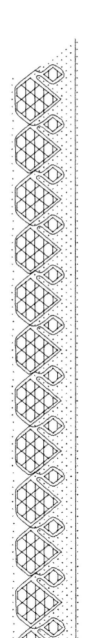

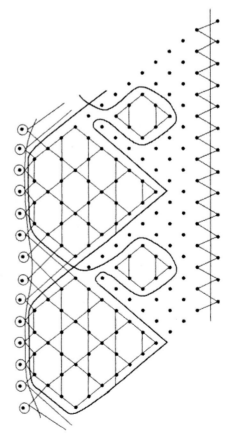

Pattern 1250-1875.9

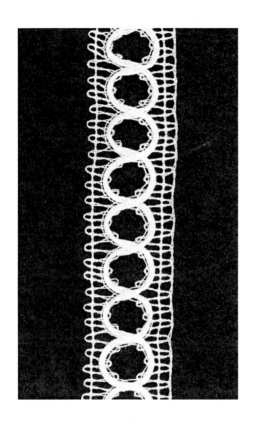

Bobbins 6 pairs

Thread Brok 120/2

Gimp DMC Coton á Broder 25
1 pair

nb. gimp bobbins are wound with the
thread doubled

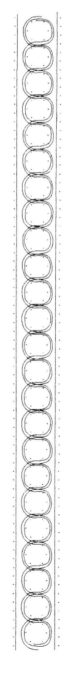

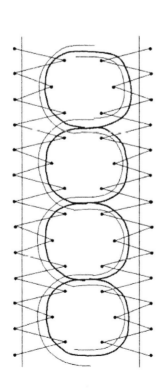

Pattern 1250-1875.12

Bobbins 11 pairs

Thread   Brok 120/2

Gimp   DMC Coton á Broder 25
             1 pair

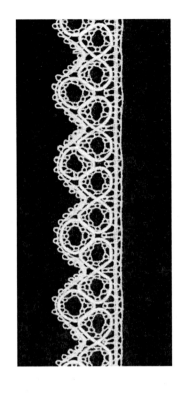

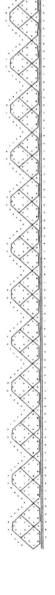

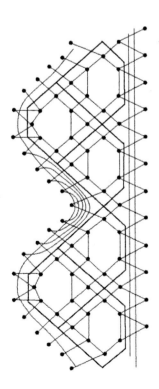

Pattern 1250-1875.17

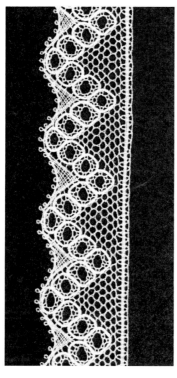

Bobbins 20 pairs

Thread Brok 120/2

Gimp DMC Coton á Broder 25
1 pair

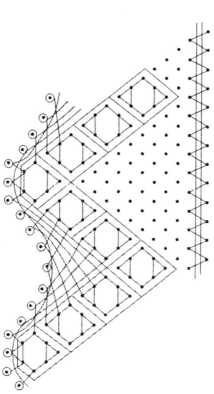

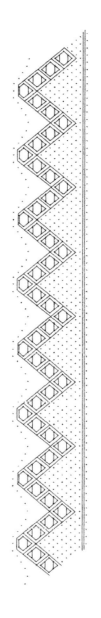

Pattern 138-1883 'The Grecian'

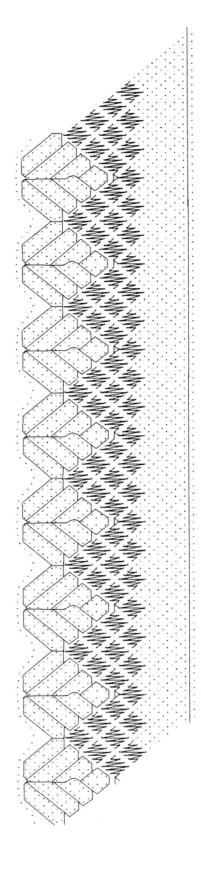

Bobbins 41 pairs

Thread Brok 120/2

Gimp DMC Coton á Broder 25
1 pair

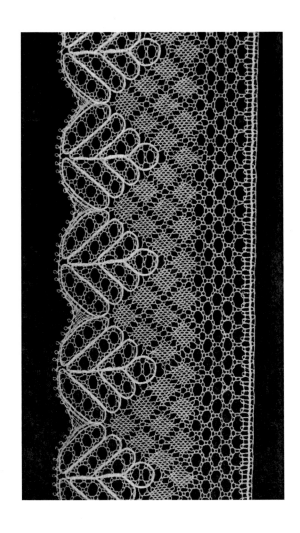

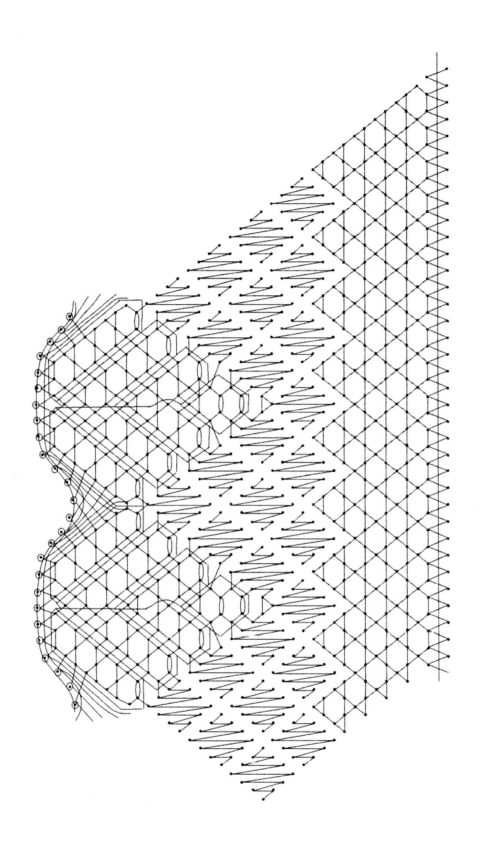

117

INDEX